Praise for *True Tales from the Campaign Trail*

Politics at its best: heartfelt, humane and humorous. *True Tales from the Campaign Trail* is a tonic, an elixir. It reminds us of what politics could be, and should be again. Pull up a chair, sit back and enjoy these laugh-out-loud stories. Like a collection of behind-the-scenes, in-the-locker-room stories from your favorite sports team, this book colorfully portrays the humanity and humor of the characters who play politics at the highest levels. Jerry Austin has captured the best of what is the essence of American politics—flawed human beings fighting hard for their beliefs, and their dreams.

—Michael Curtin, former editor of the *Columbus Dispatch* and retired state legislator

Jerry Austin has been a leader in bringing change and supporting outsiders, women, liberals, and people of color. He has been dedicated and clear about supporting real democracy. This book is a great, fun read which will keep you laughing and passing it on. It includes lots of behind the scenes looks at the events we know. At the same time Jerry really understands the core principles of campaigns, and this is a great way to learn about real politics and campaigns in a most enjoyable read.

—Celinda Lake, pollster

D1242569

Bliss Institute Series
John C. Green, Editor

Jerry Austin, *True Tales from the Campaign Trail: Stories Only Political Consultants Can Tell*

William L. Hershey and John C. Green, *Mr. Chairman: The Life and Times of Ray C. Bliss*

Douglas M. Brattebo, Tom Lansford, Jack Covarrubias, and Robert J. Pauly Jr., editors,
Culture, Rhetoric, and Voting: The Presidential Election of 2012

Douglas M. Brattebo, Tom Lansford, and Jack Covarrubias, editors,
A Transformation in American National Politics: The Presidential Election of 2012

Daniel J. Coffey, John C. Green, David B. Cohen, and Stephen C. Brooks,
Buckeye Battleground: Ohio, Campaigns, and Elections in the Twenty-First Century

Lee Leonard, *A Columnist's View of Capitol Square: Ohio Politics and Government, 1969–2005*

Abe Zaidan, with John C. Green, *Portraits of Power: Ohio and National Politics, 1964–2004*

True Tales from the Campaign Trail
Stories Only Political Consultants Can Tell

Written and compiled by Jerry Austin

Edited by Jerry Austin, Sheryl Losser, and John C. Green

University of Akron Press
Akron, Ohio

All inquiries and permission requests should be addressed to the Publisher, The University of Akron Press, Akron, Ohio 44325-1703.

ISBN: 978-1-629221-11-3 (paper)
ISBN: 978-1-629221-12-0 (ePDF)
ISBN: 978-1-629221-13-7 (ePub)

A catalog record for this title is available from the Library of Congress.

∞ The paper used in this publication meets the minimum requirements of ANSI / NISO Z39.48–1992 (Permanence of Paper).

Cover design and illustration: Doug Granger

True Tales from the Campaign Trail was designed and typeset in Adobe Caslon with Futura display by Amy Freels. *True Tales from the Campaign Trail* was printed on sixty-pound white and bound by Bookmasters of Ashland, Ohio.

Contents

Introduction   xi

I. Elections and Campaigns

San Francisco Mayor's Race | *Jerry Austin*   3

No Piña Colada Party | *Bob Keefe*   5

No French Kissing | *Bob Mulholland*   8

No One Sells Their Last Renoir | *Jeff Plaut*   10

Jesse's Plane Money | *Jerry Austin*   11

Give Us This Day, Our Daley Bread | *Frank Watkins*   14

This Guy Has No Chance of Winning | *Jim Friedman*   16

Learn to Drive Ted Kennedy | *Doc Sweitzer*   18

A Thousand Cuban Refugees | *John Rendon*   21

The Trip from Hell | *Richard Norman*   23

The Transportation Contest | *Jerry Austin*   28

Street Money | *Garry South*   31

Jumbo, the Precinct Captain | *Frank Watkins*   34

Knocking on Doors | *Tom King*   36

Don't Invest to Lose | *Tom King*   38

A Historic Election | *Jerry Austin*   41

Nothing Succeeds as Planned | *J. Warren Tompkins*   45

I Ran for Team Mascot | *Steve Cohen*   48

Advancing in Nebraska | *John Rendon*   51

Sometimes You Get Lucky | *Dale Emmons*   53

II. Political Communication

You Have to Ask for Every Vote | *Nancy Korman*   63

When Attacked, You Have to Respond | *Bob Mulholland*   64

A Powerful Message | *Rich Schlackman*   65

Texas Swagger in Vermont | *Paul Curcio*   67

The Farmer Ad | *Jerry Austin*   69

Always Go with Your Instincts | *Jerry Austin*   71

An Obvious Endorser | *Jerry Austin*   74

Gimmicks and Authenticity | *Tom Ingram*   77

Getting a Message Across | *Tom King*   79

Panda Bear | *Jerry Austin*   81

Human Radar | *Ace Smith*   83

"If We Can't Eat Them, We Shouldn't Shoot Them" | *Jeff Plaut*   85

Ash Wednesday | *John Rendon*   88

No Cameras, No Story | *Tom King*   89

You Could Not Say That, But I Could | *Jerry Austin*   91

Signs for the Times | *Bob Mulholland*   95

"Meet the New Boss. Same as the Old Boss" | *Garry South*   96

The Gang of Five | *Alice Huffman*   98

The Rise of Dick Morris | *Jerry Austin*   101

How I Became Political Director | *Paul Curcio*   103

Getting Some Guidance | *Alice Huffman*   106

Changing the Primary Date | *John Rendon*   108

Convention Madness | *Rick Rendon*   112

Convention Chaos | *Jerry Austin*   115

III. Wry and Wise

Presidential Impersonation | *Jerry Austin*   121

A Good Hand Man | *Bob Keefe*   123

The Sweepstakes | *David Heller*   125

A Pollster Not an Upholsterer | *Jeff Plaut*   127

Gary's Gorillas | *John Toohey*   128

Apologizing to Protestants | *Nancy Korman*   130

I'm Not a Puppet | *Peter Fenn*   132

Rendon, I Got Other Plans | *John Rendon*   134

A Moment with the President | *Jerry Austin*   135

Bananas | *Richard Norman*   137

Airport Security | *Steve Cobble*   139

Two Double Beds | *Garry South*   141

Celebrity for a Day | *Jerry Austin*   144

A Pizza Guy | *John Toohey*   147

Saturday Night Live | *Steve Cobble*   149

Mosquito Inspector | *Steve Murphy*   151

Are You from New Orleans? | *Tom King*   153

Jamillah | *Jerry Austin*   155

Jenrette | *Jerry Austin*   156

Humble Pie Act | *Garry South*   158

Winning the Nose Ring Vote | *Steve Cobble*   160

A Scary Invitation | *Jerry Austin*   162

IV. Leadership and Appreciation

Remembering Mo | *Karen T. Scates*   167

Meeting Ronald Reagan | *Bill Lacy*   170

Ted's Humanity | *Nancy Korman*   172

The Nuclear Codes | *Richard Norman*   174

The First Catholic Priest in Congress | *Nancy Korman*   176

Still Conservative After All These Years | *Bill Lacy*   178

A Job Interview | *Jerry Austin*   181

Branch Water and Bourbon | *Tom Ingram*   188

From Now On, He's With Me | *Howie Carroll*   190

Miss Anna Belle | *Tom Ingram*   194

Great Storyteller | *Nancy Korman*   196

A Story Left Untold | *Jerry Austin*   198

Justice and Power Politics | *Steve Cobble*   200

Coach Hayes and His Football Family | *Jerry Austin*   202

Campaigning for Lula | *Steve Cobble*   205

The Ballot Box Revolution | *Jerry Austin*   207

Comrade Steve | *Steve Cobble*   211

On the Road to Belfast | *Jerry Austin*   213

The Ostrich Has Landed | *Wayne Johnson*   219

The People Vote No | *Jerry Austin*   221

About the Contributors   225

Introduction

The concept for *True Tales from the Campaign Trail* originated with the *Chicken Soup for the Soul* series of books.

Chicken Soup consisted of inspirational true stories about ordinary people's lives. The book became an international best seller. Later, versions were published targeted for a specific demographic, i.e. *Chicken Soup for the Teenage Soul.* And to date, books in this genre have been published regularly since the first book in 1993.

True Tales is based on interviews with longtime Democratic and Republican political consultants. These consultants' stories were transcribed and edited, and are presented here for the enjoyment of those readers who enjoy politics and/or a good story.

Chicken Soup and *True Tales from the Campaign Trail* share an "you can't make this up" originality.

The first story could have been published in *Chicken Soup*: A candidate for mayor experiences a once-in-a-lifetime, unplanned moment that will be remembered in the annals of San Francisco politics forever.

The stories are divided into four sections of roughly equal length—a rough and ready division, since some stories could be in more than one section.

"Elections and Campaigns" features stories involving Jimmy Carter, Bill Clinton, and Oliver North, while "Political Communication" reports on successful—and unsuccessful—efforts to communicate with voters and politicians.

"Wry and Wise" contains accounts of the funny foibles and lessons learned. And "Leadership and Appreciation" remembers effective leaders, such Ronald Reagan and Ted Kennedy, and celebrates the virtues of the democratic process, here and abroad.

I would like to thank the fellow consultants who shared their stories; Sheryl Losser for help editing the stories; Doug Granger for designing the cover; the Bliss Institute of Applied Politics for supporting the project; and the University of Akron Press for publishing this book.

ENJOY!
Gerald "Jerry" Austin
Akron, Ohio
Summer 2017

I. Elections and Campaigns

San Francisco Mayor's Race

Jerry Austin

In 1991, I was retained as the consultant for the first Asian-born American to run for mayor of a major city.

Tom Hsieh ("Shea") was born in China and had migrated to San Francisco in the early 1950s. An architect by profession, Hsieh was the first Asian elected to the Board of Supervisors, the local government in San Francisco.

Tom Hsieh continued to have a very distinctive accent as well as a habit of speaking at times in "cookie monster" type phrases—phrases without a verb.

During the campaign, I produced an ad with Tom looking at the camera asking, "What do you want, good grammar or good government?"

The highlight of any San Francisco mayor's race is the final televised debate, scheduled in prime time on a major network. San Franciscans consider politics a contact sport. The debate always has a better-than-average-size viewing audience for a televised political event.

The major candidates were Art Agnos, the embattled incumbent; Angela Alioto, another member of the Board of Supervisors and the daughter of former mayor Joe Alioto; Frank Jordan, a former chief of police; Richard Hongisto, a former sheriff and Board of Supervisors member; and Tom Hsieh.

The televised debate took place on the Thursday before the election. I had briefed Tom that he would only have one minute to make a statement. The remainder of the debate would be Q & A. We practiced answers to possible questions. For his one-minute statement, I rehearsed him stating that "Art Agnos' homeless program was a pipe dream."

We practiced the line over and over again. Many times he left out the verb "was." Finally he had it right. I joined the other candidate staffers, including Dee Dee Myers, who was communications director for Frank Jordan, in the holding room to watch the telecast on TV.

When it came time for Hsieh to make his statement, I was confident he could deliver the one line without a hitch. He looked at the camera with a stern visage and began, "Art Agnos homeless program is a wet dream."

Everyone started laughing. Hsieh did not know what to do, so he simply grinned. When the laughter died down the moderator continued the debate.

After the conclusion of the debate, I waited for Tom to enter the holding room. He arrived and said, "Why were they laughing at me?" I said, "Tom, you were supposed to say that Art Agnos' homeless program is a pipe dream and you said 'wet dream.'" He said, "What's the difference?"

The next year during the Democratic presidential primaries, I was working for Paul Tsongas and Dee Dee Myers was working for Bill Clinton. I ran in to her at one of the debates. She looked at me, pointed her finger at me and said with a laugh, "wet dream."

No Piña Colada Party

Bob Keefe

Thanks to my good friend Bob Strauss, who was National Democratic Party chair at the time, I ended up managing Senator Henry "Scoop" Jackson's presidential campaign in 1976. It was a tough campaign year because you had eight or ten candidates on the Democratic side, all looking for an early "breakout" state. Every campaign needed an early win in the primary cycle to remain viable.

We had a problem when you look at the early primary and caucus states. Scoop was not a good fit for the Iowa caucuses because I didn't think we had the ability to organize there. Iowa had not been that significant in the past; this was the first time it was an important state. But it was a caucus state that required a lot of organizing. So we decided to skip Iowa.

Next you had New Hampshire. That state was a problem for us because, although it had a lot of more conservative Democrats, it also had a lot of weird people on the conservative side. Scoop attracted a lot of weirdos, people you just wouldn't want to walk down the street with.

So you had eight or ten candidates in the race, all struggling to get endorsements and supporters. I felt I couldn't really make a commitment to New Hampshire because we just couldn't get the people or the star power up there.

Massachusetts, however, was perfect for us. It was perfect for two reasons. It was early in the election cycle and it was tailor-made for Scoop. People didn't really understand Massachusetts. They just thought it was this bastion of liberalism. So if Scoop won Massachusetts, they'd sit up and take notice because they didn't think he'd do well up there.

We decided to make our play for Massachusetts, but the next problem was that we needed a win before that or we wouldn't make it to Massachusetts.

So I studied the primary schedule and plotted it out. Puerto Rico was having its caucuses on the Sunday *before* New Hampshire. And Puerto Rico, as it turns out, had more delegates! They had twenty delegates and New Hampshire only had sixteen.

Jackson had been the chairman of the Senate Interior Committee for many years and was known in Puerto Rico. He was actually a big deal in Puerto Rico.

Rafael Hernández Colón was the governor, chair of the Democratic Party there, and a Jackson supporter. We laid out a scenario where we would win all eight caucuses around Puerto Rico. Going into the first primary in New Hampshire we would have a lead in delegates because Iowa's delegates wouldn't be counted yet.

If the vote in New Hampshire split between several candidates then we would go into Massachusetts with a lead in delegates.

Then, along comes Franklin Delano López, causing problems for us in Puerto Rico. He was an interesting self-starter who had worked for the governor but was now working for another candidate, Jimmy Carter.

Frankie had been in politics for awhile and he decided to make a play in Puerto Rico by getting his hands on the Carter campaign and delivering a win for Carter. He would be seen as the king of Puerto Rico to the Carter folks and would advance his political career in the process.

He basically succeeded by ambushing the caucuses; I still don't have a complete report of what happened. They shut down the caucuses—there were fistfights and brawls. It was a complete mess.

So needless to say, the Piña Colada party I had planned for a hotel in Manchester, New Hampshire never happened.

We won the Massachusetts primary after New Hampshire, and we planned to have a great big victory party in New York, which was the next primary state and of course a huge media market. But there were three or four other states in play the same day as Massachusetts, and there were late counts coming in from places where Morris Udall and Carter were neck and neck.

We were stopping at the hotel, across from Central Park, and discovered there was a strike going on outside the hotel! We couldn't even get the TV crews into the building.

We ended up having our victory party in Central Park and boy was it a mess. That was sort of the way things were going in the Jackson campaign.

It all came down to Pennsylvania and we just plumb ran out of money. Pennsylvania is a big state; it takes a lot of money to compete there and we were running on fumes.

Carter had the money thing worked out because he had a way of financing the media. Bert Lance, who was a banker, would loan money to Jerry Rafshoon, the media consultant, and then Jerry would produce the ads and make the buys. The campaign would catch up on paying Jerry's invoices when more money came in and he would turn around and pay off the loan. That way they always had money for their media buys.

Carter was the only candidate to have media after the first month of the campaign in 1976 and that's how it was done.

The rest of the candidates, one by one, dropped out of the race when they eventually ran out of money.

No French Kissing

Bob Mulholland

I managed the only successful campaign to close down a nuclear power plant in the United States, the Rancho Seco plant in Sacramento, California.

Previously, there had been twelve nuclear power plant elections in the U.S. All of them lost. As I talked to the people who were involved, I realized that they all ran against radiation. You cannot win elections by running against radiation. You only get the votes of those against radiation, which is not enough to win an election.

So we changed our tactics to expose poor management of the plant. I ran the campaign based on performance-economics: the plant was fourteen years old, and over its fourteen years, it only ran at 37 percent capacity.

We found out that two of the workers in the control room were arrested for using drugs when driving. The press covered it, asking questions about whether they used cocaine while in the control room. Though our reports did not say cocaine, it was the drug they used. The media named cocaine as the drug in all their news reports. We publicized misuse of the plant manager's expense account.

I used every tactic in the book to create press and we ultimately had 53 percent of the vote. The next day the Rancho Seco plant was to be shut down forever.

But there was a little loophole that allowed firms to buy into the plant that had been closed. Then I had to counter all the attempts by other utilities to buy the plant.

A large French nuclear power company with about forty to sixty nuclear plants was one of the utilities that expressed an interest in the shutdown plant.

So I did a press conference with the sign, "No French Kissing."

My strategy was that we were not going to win unless we destroyed our opponent's reputation and it worked.

No One Sells Their Last Renoir

Jeff Plaut

I was the pollster for Mark Dayton's race for governor of Minnesota in 2010. Dayton was a former Senator and heir to the Dayton chain of department stores.

In the gubernatorial race, we had a very hotly contested Democratic primary against the speaker of the General Assembly.

Mark had spent a good deal of his own money running for Senate and pledged not to do the same in his race for governor. But he was concerned about the campaign and the fact that we weren't on TV and needed to be.

We had a lot of discussions about how to get on TV, the fact that we needed to be on TV. Basically, the campaign needed an infusion of cash.

All of a sudden we were on TV.

I asked the campaign manager how we came up with the money to buy TV time. She told me that Mark sold a Renoir painting he had, and it was going to take care of our million-dollar-plus television buy for that week.

I said, somewhat jokingly, "I don't know how many Mark has, but no one sells their *last* Renoir. Isn't there another one we can sell?"

The sale of the painting allowed us to win the primary. Mark went on to be elected governor of Minnesota.

Jesse's Plane Money

Jerry Austin

Jesse Jackson was the first Democratic presidential candidate in 1988 to lease a plane. The plane was first used after the Iowa caucuses, but the research and negotiations took place months before.

Our plan was to have a plane available after the Iowa caucuses because the next meaningful contest was Super Tuesday, March 20, 1988. On this date twenty states would hold primaries and caucuses. The states were mostly in the south but also included Massachusetts, Missouri, Maryland, and Washington.

The economics of leasing a plane were very sobering. I found a plane broker in St. Louis who had a list of hundreds of planes available for use. I needed a plane with at least one hundred seats. The first price I was quoted was $600,000 per month with a one-month security deposit. So I needed a total of $1.2 million, which I did not have nor did I ever expect to have. I told the broker that was too much and asked if he could do better. He said he'd get back to me.

A week later he called and said he had a plane with all of my requirements except a galley. The owner very much wanted to garner the publicity of having one of his planes used by a presidential candidate and was willing to come down in price. He wanted $320,000 per month with a month's security deposit. I told the broker that we had a plane, smaller than we needed, but the price was right. It was owned by a

Saudi friend of Reverend Jackson. The upside was the price, $150,000 per month. The downside was that Saudi would need the plane from time to time. This was problematic.

The broker asked what I was willing to pay. I responded, "$320,000 per month in eight payments of $40,000 and no security deposit." He told me he had to check with the owner and would have an answer within twenty-four hours.

I told Jackson of my negotiations and he asked which Saudi friend offered the plane. I told him there was no friend. I made it up.

I knew that the press corps would be travelling with us leading up to Super Tuesday and beyond if we were successful. In addition, the Secret Service would also occupy several seats on the plane. I was allowed to charge the press corps and the Secret Service 125 percent of a first-class ticket as their fare for riding on the plane and for the transportation we would also provide.

Raising the eight payments of $40,000 was a 1988 version of the Civil Rights movement of the 1960s. Civil rights workers would travel by car from county to county and state to state. At each location they would pass the hat to raise enough money to put gas in the car to get to the next place.

We needed to fund raise the same way in 1988—raise enough money to put fuel in the plane to get to the next event.

The schedule began to include two and sometimes three fundraising events each day. Most of these events were held at black churches. Jackson would always end his speech with an appeal for money, but the majority of these audiences were poor people. Most of them were on welfare and were female heads of households.

He would always start his appeal by asking who would give $1,000, the legal limit. He would keep lowering the denomination until he asked, "Who would give something?" All the hands were raised. We had preprinted envelopes that were handed out. The audience put their donation in the envelope and we collected them and quickly left the church.

I was always confronted by local supporters who wanted the money we raised to stay in their community to help defray their costs. I needed the money to pay for the plane. In order to avoid a physical confrontation, I would find a private office to count the money, bundle it in stacks of $100 and transport it back to the bank in Chicago.

The overwhelming denomination we received was $1 bills. Once in awhile we'd come across a $5 bill. These donors were welfare recipients. A dollar to them was a good deal of money. Many wrote personal notes on the envelopes. Usually these notes stated, "All my prayers are with you" or "I'm sorry this is all I can afford."

After bundling the money, I did something unadvisable. I sent the money, sometimes thousands of dollars in cash, back to Chicago via Federal Express. Over the course of the campaign, we sent over $1 million back to Chicago that way.

It is important to remember that in those days for the Federal Election Commission provided matching funds for primary candidates—dollar per dollar up to the first $250 per donor. A suburbanite could write a check for $25 and with the match it would become $50.

But a cash contribution was not matchable—only checks or money orders. So a welfare recipient could not have his contribution doubled by giving cash. The theory was that someone could give people cash to contribute. This would be a vehicle for someone who had given the max to avoid the limit by giving cash that was then re-donated by these poor people. The Jackson campaign did not have the luxury of $1,000 donors who would give additional cash. Besides, it was against the rules.

Over the course of the campaign, the Jackson for President Committee raised over $29 million in donations and matching funds. Over $3 million of the $29 million was donated in cash and therefore was never matched.

Give Us This Day, Our Daley Bread

Frank Watkins

I was hired by Reverend Jesse Jackson on the day that Operation PUSH (People United to Save Humanity) was founded—December 25, 1971. I had been a volunteer at Operation Breadbasket for several years until I was hired by PUSH. I started off as the "Suburban Coordinator" organizing white folks in the Chicago suburbs.

We were doing hunger programs and food distribution centers, so to raise money I would get suburban churches and synagogues to donate food to the food pantries. Making hunger illegal was one of our priorities—that's how I got into politics.

One of the most interesting things that happened during this time had to do with a politician named Claude Holman. He was alderman and the Democratic committeeman in the 4th Ward, which was where PUSH was located. Holman was a staunch supporter of Chicago Mayor Richard J. Daley—and African American.

Holman was the most loyal machine politician of them all. Daley would come to meet with the ministers and Holman would have the opening prayer, and it was "give us this day, our Daley bread."

We wanted to beat him, so we worked in the 4th Ward for Bill Cousins, Jr., the only black alderman who was independent of the machine. We registered two thousand new voters, but Holman removed four thousand voters from the registration list by using *show cause notices*.

The *show cause notice* system worked like this. On the Tuesday, four weeks before the election, you could register to vote in your local precinct. Then on that Thursday and Friday, the Democratic and Republican precinct captains would go around the ward, and if there was a vacant lot where there were supposed to be registered voters or if you questioned someone's registration, you turned that in to the Board of Election commissioners. They would then send a notice, a *show cause notice*, stating "unless you show cause that we should not remove you from the rolls, your name will be removed."

Since there were no Republicans in Chicago, basically the Democratic precinct captains would go around, and if you weren't a voter they could count on, it was one of the ways they would harass you. They would turn your name in so that you would get *a show cause notice*.

You then had to go all the way downtown to the Board of Elections and prove that you were a registered voter and that your voting address was correct. This was used as a deterrent to voters in many parts of Chicago.

We had a game plan to register two thousand new voters and he had a counter-game plan to take four thousand voters off the rolls. So it was a losing proposition. We couldn't defeat him: for every voter we added, he took two voters away.

This Guy Has No Chance of Winning

Jim Friedman

I didn't get involved in the 1976 Birch Bayh for President primary campaign until November of 1975. All the other candidates were already running at full speed. It was like trying to catch a runaway freight train.

The 1976 campaign was the first post-Watergate election psychologically, politically, and legally. It was the first election where there were federal matching funds and contribution limits. The rules had all changed so we had a terrible time just trying to comply with the Federal Elections Commission (FEC) and keep the records for the contributions—let alone raise the money.

That November, December and January, I kept hearing people saying, "This guy Jimmy Carter, who is this guy Carter, why is he running? He doesn't have a chance." Part of that skepticism was just Washington-centric attitude. Almost everybody else who was in the race was a U.S. senator, except this unknown governor from Georgia.

I first met Carter right after the general election in 1970. I was involved with John "Jack" Gilligan, who was elected governor of Ohio. A significant number of other new Democratic governors were also elected that year, including Jimmy Carter.

The National Governors Association held a seminar for the new governors, right after the election, on "How to Be a Governor." They brought in other Democratic governors and their staffs to hold sessions on governing.

The seminar took place at Pinehurst Resort in North Carolina. So Jack and his wife Katie, my wife Ruth and I all fly down to the resort in an Ohio National Guard Plane. One morning Ruth comes back from breakfast and says, "You know I just met the most charming, fascinating guy, he's really a terrific person. He's the new governor of Georgia."

I looked at her and said, "Ruth, I'm sure he's a very nice guy. But this guy has no future. Don't you realize the governor of Georgia can't even run for reelection? He may be a very nice guy, but you'll never hear from him again."

In 1974, Bob Strauss from Texas became the National Finance Chair for the Democratic National Committee (DNC) and I was appointed vice chair of the committee. In the summer of 1975, the finance committee was invited to go to Los Angeles to participate in a telethon to raise money for the DNC. After the telethon there was a big party at the home of Lew Wasserman, head of Universal Studios, Cleveland native, and huge Democratic fundraiser.

So who shows up at the party? Jimmy Carter.

Carter comes over to me to say hello and I say, "Hey, governor, how are you?"

Carter says, "Well, I'm running for president."

I think to myself—sure, yeah, okay—because every candidate who gets elected plans on running for president someday.

But I was nice and just responded, "Okay Governor. If you're coming to Ohio give me a call and let me know."

A few weeks later, I'm back in Cleveland, and I come back from lunch to find a pink call slip saying, "Jimmy Carter called."

I said to my secretary, "I'm not calling because I know what he wants. He wants me to go out and raise money for him and this guy's got *absolutely* no chance of winning."

Three months later Carter won the Iowa caucuses, Bayh dropped out after finishing third in New Hampshire, and I ended up on the road for soon-to-be President Jimmy Carter.

Learn to Drive Ted Kennedy

Doc Sweitzer

During the Democratic presidential primary in 1980 Senator Ted Kennedy was running against President Jimmy Carter, and both campaigns were participating in the Florida caucuses.

The Florida caucuses were always a really big deal. I was working for the Kennedy campaign and I knew Florida so I asked, "Can I go and work on the caucuses down in Florida?"

I had worked in Palm Beach the prior two years on a congressional race and had also worked in an ad agency down there. So I was familiar with the area. The campaign agreed to my request and I flew down to Palm Beach, getting in around eleven a.m. midweek.

I went directly to the Kennedy headquarters and finally found it on a second-story floor above a jewelry store in Palm Beach—a location that no one would ever find if they were just driving by.

It was in a cramped room with one hardline phone. There were about a dozen adults standing around. I was in my twenties at the time and the people in the headquarters were all older and more experienced. They were mostly union officials and political activists out of Washington, DC, who were down there trying to pull this event together.

They were miserable because they had no space and no phones. After seeing their predicament, I said, "Listen, I'll go locate a new headquarters. I know the area. Give me a driver and I'll take care of it."

So I left with a driver and we start driving around West Palm Beach until I spotted an empty building with a storefront that I knew had been the campaign headquarters for Governor Bob Graham. It was a great location.

I walked in and asked the owner if we could use the space for two weeks for the caucuses. He said, "Absolutely, you can use it. No problem."

I told him, "We have to pay you something for the use of the space," and he said, "Just give us $300 or something."

We now had a campaign headquarters in a great location in West Palm Beach. I just had to get phones and it's already two o'clock in the afternoon, and there I am, going through the yellow pages, because I don't know who to call. Who do you call to get phones put in fast at two o'clock in the afternoon?

I decided to call the president of Southern Bell in Atlanta. Somehow I got the guy on the phone and I explained the situation to him: "I'm working in this presidential campaign. I need hardline phones and I need them now. Can you help me out?"

The guy said, "We'll get on it" and hung up. By five o'clock they were throwing hard lines into the headquarters and the technicians said, "I don't know who you are buddy but they pulled us from a commercial job to come over here and put these phones in—so we're going to put these phones in."

By ten o'clock all the phones were in and I was told they would be fully operational in something like eight hours.

The next day I show up at the new headquarters with all the union officials and political activists in tow to show off our new space. We're walking and we notice there is a photographer outside, so I go running out to figure out what the heck is going on.

It turns out the guy is from the *National Inquirer* and he takes some photographs, and then runs off when he sees us.

We're just standing there staring at our new sign that says "Ted Kennedy for President" outside the headquarters. I can't figure out why that photographer would be shooting photos of the front of our headquarters. Finally my eyes drifted upwards and it dawned on me that there was a sign right above ours.

I had accidentally rented a vacant building that used to be a driving studio, where you go to learn to drive, and there was a huge sign above ours that said, "Learn to Drive."

Since our sign was right below, it now read "Learn to Drive Ted Kennedy" and below that it just said, "For President."

He was taking a picture because of the irony of a driving studio for Kennedy headquarters and the words "Learn to Drive." It looked like a reference to Kennedy's automobile accident in Chappaquiddick back in 1969.

What a message—"Learn to Drive Ted Kennedy"—

I sort of crashed right then and there. I thought "I'm done. My career in politics is over. I can't recover from this."

I figured I had really damaged my reputation and I certainly wasn't going to be involved in campaigns the rest of my life. I'd be lucky if anyone would let me volunteer. I would be seen as a complete failure.

The folks that were in the headquarters, however, were all more experienced than I was and they realized it was just another one of those up-and-down moments we all go through in campaigns. They knew things like this always happen.

They figured there would be a one-day story about it in the *National Inquirer*. It was not the end of the world.

They all tried to cheer me up saying, "Listen, we all missed it. We all walked right by it. These things happen. *The important thing at the moment is that we now have a real headquarters and we have phones.*"

Years later I would realize just how appropriate their response was. Campaigns will have ups and downs on a daily basis. You just have to roll with it.

A Thousand Cuban Refugees

John Rendon

About a year after the 1980 Carter presidential campaign I'm in Florida at a Jefferson-Jackson Day dinner for the Florida Democratic Party and they're roasting Bob Strauss, former chairman of the Democratic National Committee.

Bill Clinton is at the roast and tells this story about Strauss from the 1980 campaign.

Strauss was the chairman of Carter's reelection campaign and then-Arkansas Governor Bill Clinton was active in the reelection bid. A rising star in the party, Clinton had dealt with some controversial issues, including the Mariel boatlift, a mass exodus of Cuban refugees to the United States, including Arkansas.

So Strauss calls Clinton one day to discuss the campaign and says,

"Now, Governor, this president of the United States, seeking the highest office in the land, has decided some young governor by the name of William Jefferson Clinton, needs to go get all the other governors to support his reelection bid against the senior Senator from the Commonwealth of Massachusetts, Edward Mora Kennedy. Are you going to accept this job?"

Clinton starts negotiating a little bit and Strauss says, *"Whatever you want—whatever you want—roads, bridges—whatever you want."*

Clinton goes off to start making phone calls and gets all but one of the Democratic governors on board.

Later Strauss calls him back after some time has passed and says, "Well, how'd you do?"

Clinton says, "Well, I got all of 'em but one."

Strauss was pulling his chain at this point and said, "All but one?"

Clinton responded "Yeah—now what about all of those roads and bridges?"

Strauss then says, "Clinton, I can't get you those roads and bridges, but I can send you one thousand Cuban refugees."

The Trip from Hell

Richard Norman

The first candidate that I ever really got to know personally was Oliver (Ollie) North.

Ollie was in the Reagan administration on the National Security Council. He gained notoriety during the Iran-Contra scandal—where the United States sold weapons to Iran and diverted the proceeds to the Contra rebel groups in Nicaragua. He was in televised hearings before Congress and was later acquitted in court of all the charges brought against him.

We first got to know Ollie during the time that his appeal was in the courts. There was a legal defense fund and we were brought in to do fundraising for the fund. We raised a significant amount of money. After the acquittal, North started a 501(c)3 charitable foundation called Freedom Alliance, which is still around today. It is quite a significant organization that is best known for the scholarships they give to war veterans of the Iraq War.

Ollie then resigned from Freedom Alliance in 1993 to start his campaign for the U.S. Senate in Virginia in 1994. But the fundraising did not go well. In his first nine months he only raised about $500,000. There was a revolt among the consultants and campaign staff, and it was decided they needed to bring someone in who knew how to raise big chunks of money.

I took a leave of absence from my company and started fundraising full time for the Ollie North for Senate campaign in December of 1993. Over the next ten months we raised over $24 million which, at the time, was the most money ever raised for a U.S. Senate campaign.

During that time I oversaw all aspects of fundraising and I also traveled a lot with Ollie because he was flying across the country for fundraising events.

Ollie had a unique set of circumstances to deal with due to his notoriety. Everyone recognized him because the congressional hearings had been televised. He couldn't walk through an airport without security because people either loved him or hated him.

People who hated him would try to attack him and people who loved him would run up to him, hug him, and want him to autograph their forehead. It was crazy the way people responded to his personality back then, so we always had security with us.

There was one particular trip that was very memorable. We were going to Seattle, Washington, for a series of four fundraisers. There was a private luncheon, a book signing for his book at a Christian book store, followed by a private event at someone's home, and a Washington state Republican Party event for 2,500 people where he was the keynote speaker.

These events were planned before I came on board and they had hired a local freelance fundraiser to put them together. All I knew was that I had to get Ollie out there for the long schedule of events and then we were taking the red eye home—so it was a brutal twenty-four hours.

That morning we met at the Dulles airport about eight a.m. to get on our flight to Denver. Denver was having a snowstorm, so we were late arriving and we missed our plane to Seattle. Finally they get us on another flight but our schedule was screwed up because we were running about two hours late getting to Seattle.

The luncheon became a midafternoon snack but all the people were very good about the change. It was at someone's house and we had a good crowd of people—

about one hundred people and they were all business people—so I expected to walk out of the event with around $100,000.

After we left, I asked the event organizer, who I had only spoken with once or twice by phone, "How much money did we raise?" And he said, "Well you know that really wasn't a fundraiser," and he starts talking in circles trying to explain why it wasn't a *fundraiser*. I finally said, "What are you saying?" He said, "Well, we didn't raise anything there."

So we brought our candidate all the way across the country to what was supposed to be a fundraiser and we raised nothing.

The book signing was next on the schedule. There were people wrapped all the way around the building—there must have been one thousand people waiting to get their book signed. Ollie was great about signing his autograph because it was so fast. He could sign the book, have a picture taken and be done in about fifteen seconds.

I noticed this strange-looking guy in the line who didn't look like everyone else. There is a particular look to people who come to a Christian bookstore to get a book signed and this guy did not look the part. He looked like one of these anarchist types. He had on a long black coat, long black flowing hair, and he kind of looked like the devil.

So as he got closer everyone was whispering "watch out for this guy." As soon as he stepped up to the table, he reached in his pocket, pulled out a dead rat, slammed it down on the table, and started shouting obscenities.

Dave, the lead security guy, and four of the Washington state police grabbed him. They picked him up and carried him right out of the bookstore. This all happened in about five seconds. This guy is being carried out the door and Ollie was just unflappable.

We finished the book signing and when we got in the car, I asked the guy, "We didn't raise any money there either right?" He said, "No that really wasn't supposed to be a fundraiser." "Okay. What's next?" He said, "Well there is a private reception at the home of the man who owns the bookstore chain. He is very wealthy and from

Virginia and we think that he and his family will all max out to the campaign. We could be looking at $100,000."

So we got to this man's house and we sit and have tea, we talk and he's very nice, we have a wonderful conversation. Ollie even asked him, "We would love to have your financial support if you could help us out with the campaign because it's very expensive."

He said, "I will consider that." So we walk out and I say, "We didn't get any money there either right?" and the guy says, "No."

I'm starting to realize that we were being scammed by this local event guy. He was not a fundraiser at all. He basically brought Ollie out to Washington state, at campaign expense, to make himself look important to all these people.

The next stop on the schedule was the large Republican Party event. We arrived at this huge auditorium with 2,500 people and we were in this little holding room when several people from the state Republican Party came in to brief us on the event.

I said, "Now listen folks, here's the deal, Ollie and I flew all the way across the country today to raise money for his campaign. He's running for the Senate and he needs people out there who are expecting to hear Ollie North. I'm not going to let him go out there and speak. You have to come up with a way that we are going to raise money for this man's campaign or I am going to take him out to the airport and we are going back to Virginia tonight and he is not going to speak and you're going to have to explain to those 2,500 people why you have no Ollie North here."

They said, "You can't do that! You can't do that!" I said, "Watch me." They said, "Well what do you want us to do?" I said, "You figure it out because this is your event."

So we got a little room, put up a backdrop and some flags. Then they go out into the hallway and announce that anyone who contributes $100 to the campaign gets a photo op and a signed book from Ollie North. They proceeded to bring in around five hundred people, one at a time, who were willing to pay the $100. They just hadn't been asked.

I said, "The second thing is I want someone to go to Quick Copy and print some envelopes and we're going to put North for Senate on them and pass them out."

We were going to give these people the opportunity to give—and when we did—they gave.

This whole trip had been the trip from hell. And it wasn't over yet.

Ollie was at the head table and they had this giant banner across the top saying it was the Republican Party Annual Gala. Right before Ollie stood up to speak, I saw the banner falling. It was a sign about one hundred feet long and about six feet tall that went all across the stage. It started to fall at one end and in slow motion started to peel down across the stage. The whole apparatus was going to crash down onto the head table. It was hitting people on the head as it fell. It was built on a wooden frame and Ollie was right under it.

Dave, the security guy, runs over and puts his hand up to catch it before it hits Ollie on the head.

Once again, Ollie was unflappable. He just got up and gave his speech. He was great and we made about $12,000 from passing the hat.

So we get back to the plane, and I said, "I don't know what to say, I'm so sorry."

He said, "You don't worry about it. It was a learning experience for all of us."

He was just the most reasonable and most understanding person I have ever worked with.

The Transportation Contest

Jerry Austin

In 1979, I was hired by the Carter/Mondale campaign to work the Florida caucuses. This was a non-binding straw vote that was started by Carter in 1975 to prove that he could beat George Wallace. The vote took place in one polling place in each county. It was a total public relations gimmick.

Senator Ted Kennedy decided to use the same strategy against incumbent President Jimmy Carter. His objective was to beat or have a strong showing against Carter.

I was assigned to Palm Beach County—the largest county geographically in the state.

I arrived at the West Palm Beach Airport and was met by a staffer who introduced herself and asked, "Are you Jewish?" I answered, "Yes," and then I said, "No, not the condos." The West Palm Beach, Boynton Beach, and Delray Beach were havens for transplanted and retired New York Jews. I was familiar with the area because my mother's family retired to Delray Beach.

I was assigned to the condos. After a few visits, I decided I needed a major Jewish politician to be the guest speaker at a meeting to be held in one of the banquet rooms at the largest condo in West Palm. I wanted Bob Strauss, the former Democratic National Committee chair and close advisor to the president.

Since Palm Beach County was important and Kennedy had targeted this county, my request for Strauss was approved.

On the day of the meeting, Strauss flew in accompanied by Terry O'Connell, a mutual friend. Terry was a Vietnam vet who had lost an eye and a hand during the war. He wore a patch over the eye and had a hook on his hand.

Strauss was magnificent. He did not lose his cool when he was asked very specific questions about how many planes the United States had sold to Jordan. It seemed that many in the audience knew each and every plane's serial number.

Near the end of his speech an elderly woman walked over to me and asked if I was with Mr. Strauss. I answered, "Yes." She pointed to the right wall and asked who that person was leaning against the wall, wearing a yarmulke, patch over his eye and a hook on his hand. I looked over and saw Terry O'Connell.

I responded, "That's the son of Moshe Dayan"—a famous Israeli general who also wore an eye patch. She responded immediately, "I didn't know one eye was hereditary."

I relayed the story to Strauss and O'Connell on the way to Worth Avenue, West Palm's trendy fashion street, where Strauss visited his favorite men's shop. They had a good laugh—especially O'Connell.

The Florida caucuses also proved to be a logistical challenge. How do you transport your supporters to one location in the entire county during a very limited time period?

The Carter folks leased every bus in the state for the day. The Kennedy forces relied on taxis and vans. It was also important to provide food for these caucus voters. Kennedy was serving bagels and lox. I cut a deal with "Charlie Chicken" to provide roasted chicken box lunches.

On the day of the caucus, Palm Beach County was hit by a torrential downpour. The parking lot was full of buses, taxis, and vans.

The procedure was to get off the bus and line up to receive a voting number. After receiving the number, the voters would have to wait until their number was called.

While my buses were in the parking lot, I went into the polling area and liberated five hundred voting numbers. I distributed them to the folks on the buses. When their number was called they exited the bus and went in to vote.

The powers that be could not figure out how these voters received their numbers because the sign-in table did not have them listed as registering.

The Carter forces won the transportation contest, tied for the lead in the food contest; but lost the vote not to Kennedy but to a nonaffiliated labor slate. The labor folks drove themselves to vote and went home to eat afterwards.

Rarely in politics has so much money been spent on a meaningless exercise in transportation and food maneuvers—General Moshe Dayan would have been proud.

Street Money

Garry South

After working in the Carter presidential campaign in 1976, I went back to Washington, DC, and became the Midwest Regional Finance Director for the Democratic National Committee (DNC). I had thirteen states from Ohio to Montana—they threw in Montana because I was from there. I was responsible for high-dollar fundraising; most of the fundraising was done in the big cities like Milwaukee, Chicago, and Indianapolis.

Then at the end of the year in 1977, the White House political office asked me to go out to Illinois to run a U. S. Senate race against incumbent Republican Chuck Percy, who they badly wanted to defeat.

I was only twenty-seven years old, I'm only two years out of Montana, and all of a sudden I'm sitting in the middle of Chicago running a senate campaign against a well-known Republican incumbent.

My candidate on the Democratic side was Alex Seith, who had never run for political office before. His political involvement had been limited to appointed positions, most notably the Cook County Zoning Board of Appeals.

Mayor Richard Daley had died at the end of 1976 and Mike Bilandic was his handpicked successor. Bilandic was Croatian-American and bland by Chicago standards. He ended up getting defeated by Jane Byrne in 1979.

One of Mayor Daley's sons, Bill, became my "minder" in Chicago. The Democratic machine didn't really care who the senate candidate was, they just didn't want us to come in and mess it up.

Bill Daley and I started having weekly breakfast meetings at the Chicago Athletic Association where Bill would give me feedback from *the guys*. Daley would say, "The *guys* think you need to…the *guys* are saying…the *guys* you want…."

I'd say, "Just who are *these guys*?" but I never got an answer. They were just nameless, faceless *guys* who were pulling the strings.

The city of Chicago has fifty wards and then there are thirty wards representing the townships outside of Chicago. Those eighty ward committeemen comprise the Cook County Central Committee.

One day Alex Seith and I went out to meet with this young Italian committeeman from Proviso Township. This was classic Cook County politics—the meeting was held in the back room of an Italian restaurant. Word got back to me after the meeting that the committeeman had been told by the Democratic organization that they didn't want him to run again for township committeeman, they wanted somebody else to run.

Apparently he told them to "f— off," he was going to run anyway, which he did. Three months later he was found dead, stuffed in the trunk of his Mercedes Benz, out on the off ramp to the Dan Ryan expressway.

I'm watching all this happen and I'm still just a babe in the woods, but that was my introduction to politics Chicago-style.

My most embarrassing incident from that campaign came when all these black ministers and bishops wanted to come in and meet with me. We had already won the primary against several opponents, so at this point we're the Democratic nominee.

And, you know, I'm new to this, I mean I've run campaigns in Montana, but what do I know about running campaigns in Chicago?

The campaign office was in an old historic building downtown right off the "L" in the southern part of the Loop. So I told my secretary, who was actually the niece of Richie Daley's wife, to set up a meeting with all these black bishops and ministers who kept asking to meet with me. They parade into my office and they're kind of hemmin' and hawin' around and I'm just sittin' there, this white kid from Montana.

Finally they start talking about why they wanted to meet with me, stating that they wanted to discuss street money. Now, *I swear to god I had no idea what they were talking about.* I'd never heard the term before. I was totally unfamiliar with walkin' around money, street money, or anything like that—money for paying campaign workers to get out the vote on election day.

So I let them ramble on while I try to figure out what's going on. Finally one of them says to me, "Uh, well, I think we're gonna need about $270,000 in street money, and we're gonna need uh...we gotta get that money movin' right away...that street money."

I said, "I'm a little confused. We're running a campaign for the United States Senate, *if you need money to fix the streets, you need to go to your alderman.*"

They looked at me like I was from a different planet.

I finally figured it out and they got their *street money.*

Jumbo, the Precinct Captain

Frank Watkins

In 1972, I was out campaigning for a candidate in the alderman's race for the 42nd Ward in Chicago. I'm in a building elevator when the elevator doors open and Burt Natarus gets in. He was our opponent in the race.

I don't remember what I was doing in that particular building and I didn't know who Burt Natarus was when he got on the elevator. But we're both in this elevator and I was wearing a button for his opponent.

He doesn't know me from Adam and I don't know who he is, but he reaches across the elevator and rips my button off, just jerks it right off my jacket. I would only find out later who the guy was.

So on election day I'm working a precinct in the 42nd ward. I had to stay until the polls closed, collect the vote count, and report any voting problems. I arrived about an hour before the polls close. I'm observing and making sure all the procedures are followed. And I plan to stay until they close down for the vote count so I can call it in to the campaign.

This big old guy, he's like six foot five, must have weighed 285 pounds—you couldn't miss him—starts harassing me. I don't know who he is, but he's clearly threatening me. As it gets closer and closer to seven o'clock, he ups the ante, and finally, about ten minutes to seven—which was when the polls close—he tells me to leave the polling place.

I tell him, "No. I'm here to do the count." I was really still in that young innocent stage, not quite sure of my rights, but not about to be bullied. I'm just a good American trying to do my duty.

I keep insisting that "I'm staying for the count."

And he keeps insisting, "No you're not, you're leaving."

"No, I'm staying."

"No. You're leaving."

We're in a verbal standoff when he charges me!

He's going to physically throw me out of the place! I stand my ground. I'm not going to take him on, but I'm NOT leaving. Finally a policeman steps in and prevents him from grabbing me, but he makes me leave the polling place.

I just sneak right back in before the polls close and I stay there, feet planted, until they close down.

After the whole thing is over, the guy comes up to me and says, "You're a tough kid, you're all right."

The next day, I'm telling everybody about this experience while I'm flipping through the *Chicago Sun Times*. I turn to page five, and there's a picture of someone underneath the curtain helping a voter cast his ballot. It was the same guy!

It was definitely the precinct I was working and a picture had been taken of this guy under the curtain helping somebody to vote. Turns out he was a renowned precinct captain known only as "Jumbo" in Chicago political circles.

So that was my first experience working a polling place in *Chicago* on election day.

Knocking on Doors

Tom King

In 1971, I was nineteen, still in college, and looking for a job for the summer like a lot of college kids in Boston. At the time there was a mayor's race going on between incumbent Mayor Kevin White and Louise Day Hicks, who was then a member of Congress.

Louise Day Hicks had taken a strong anti-desegregation position when she was on the Boston School Board. The racial thing really bothered me. Her slogan was "You know where I stand," which was code for standing up against African Americans.

Growing up in Irish Catholic West Roxbury you never met anybody that wasn't Irish Catholic. There was one kid who was half Canadian and half Italian. One black kid named Nat Butler. And the Jewish kids that we played basketball against. It was the Jews versus the Catholics on Saturday mornings down at Heinz Field. It was a fairly homogenous community, and that's what I knew. Until I went to Latin school, which was thirty percent Jewish, minority, Asian, Black, Hispanic—a melting pot. So I gained some sensitivity to racism and minority issues.

Kevin's people called me up and said, "Hey, we got a job and we think you should volunteer for it." After thinking about it, I decided to volunteer. My first job was to go out to headquarters in Ward 20. I showed up and Michael Greeley, the coordinator, hands me a list and says, "Go out and get some nomination papers signed in Ward 20, Precinct 6"—which was where I grew up.

The first day was a Saturday morning. I knock on the first door and a woman answers the door. I say, as I had been trained to do, "Would you like to sign the petition papers for the reelection of Kevin White?" She loved Kevin and signed it.

Next person, I knock on the door and the guy says, "Oh I love Kevin!" I ask, "Anybody else home?" Guy says, "Yeah, let me get my wife—come here sign for Kevin!" So far, everything's going smoothly.

The third person wasn't home. The fourth person was a woman watering her lawn and I'll never forget this as long as I live. I said, "Would you like to sign the petition papers for the reelection of Kevin White?"

She turned the water on me, got me right in the face, soaked me, and said, "I hate that son-of-a-bitch Mayor Black"—which was what some people had labeled him because he was the first mayor to admit there was a racial discrimination problem in Boston.

I quickly decided to become a precinct captain as opposed to knocking on doors.

Don't Invest to Lose

Tom King

I managed my first campaign in 1982. I was thirty-one years old and had just gotten married. Somebody working in a congressional race in Virginia told me, "You ought to go down and see this guy."

The candidate was Norman Sisisky, a Democratic state delegate from Petersburg, Virginia. Sisisky was one of the wealthiest people in the state legislature. He was challenging incumbent Congressman Bob Daniel, a Republican.

I flew down to Virginia and when I walked in to meet with him, his first question was, "Why should you run the campaign?"

So I asked him why he was running. He said, "I want to become a sex symbol." I knew he was just testing me to see how I'd react. So I said, "That's not a bad reason."

He looked at me like, "Well, he's got a sense of humor. I can deal with him."

Then he said the real reason was, "The country's been great to me and I want to give something back. I'm getting out of my business and turning it over to my son. And now I want to run for Congress."

I told him, "I'll do it."

We get our first poll results back and the race is 65 percent to 15 percent—Norman is at 15 percent. He's got about 4 percent name recognition.

My reaction was "Hmmm. Tough."

We're going through the numbers and he says, "I still think I can win."

"I think there's one way you can win," I said. "You have to get real lucky. See this black vote here that's supporting Bob Daniel; your opponent isn't going to be there in the end. Now none of them know you yet, so they're not supporting you. But he's really at 53–54."

I continued with, "I think given the situation here and the way the economy is going, and with Reagan's numbers coming back down and the economy in the tank, you've got a shot."

So we move forward. He campaigns full-out and puts in a bunch of his own money. He doesn't like to raise money because he doesn't like to ask people to give to his campaign. He has asked for money for every other cause in the world. He was the most generous son-of-a-gun I've ever dealt with. I mean he gave more money away than anybody in the world even though he was a tough businessman.

He told me one time, "Never invest in any deal when someone says to do it because you can write it off on your taxes. That's the dumbest reason. You invest money to make money."

I'll always remember that, "Don't invest in something to lose. What are you nuts!? This is business—you make money! Then you pay your taxes."

Norman was also Jewish. Almost nobody elected in the south was Jewish.

So Norman goes out and campaigns like crazy from March until August. He's a big guy and a great campaigner—people loved him when they met him.

And he thinks he's winning the race, he's thinking, "Next poll I'm gonna be even."

We get another poll back and now it's 58 percent to 20 percent, and his name recognition has increased to 7 or 8 percent—the voters still don't know who he is.

The reason he's getting 20 percent is because he's the Democrat. The reason Daniel's percentage dropped is because Reagan's numbers dropped.

Norman's reaction was, "God—I've campaigned—I've worked my tail off—What more can I do?!"

So we agreed, "Let's go on TV."

Mike McClister was handling the media. McClister's a lunatic but a good guy. So he comes in and we shoot a TV commercial, which is how I learned how to do the shooting and editing.

McClister says, "We have this clip and I want to show it to you."

In the clip, Sisisky says, "I gotta tell you, whether I'm a Democrat or a Republican, if the President is right I'm going to support him, but if he's wrong I'm going to vote against him."

He obviously misspoke. He meant to say he would vote the way district wanted and not the way the party wanted.

I said, "That says Independent to me."

McClister says, "You're right. But a lot of people are going to criticize this ad because you don't say I'm a Democrat; you say I'm not going to tell you whether I'm a Democrat or a Republican."

"Yeah, but I like it. It works."

So we decide to run the ad and Sisisky moves up in the polls but he's still losing. We get it up to 52 percent to 34 percent—something like that. Then it becomes 48 percent to 40 percent. Then all of a sudden I realize, "We're gonna win this thing. The black vote still hasn't broken our way."

On election day, we win with 55 percent. Everybody was shocked when he won because Norman was so far behind when we started.

I learned something in that campaign about black voters, about advertising and strategy, about not going on the air too early. All of those things became a part of how I view political campaigns.

A Historic Election

Jerry Austin

It's one week before the primary and both papers' polls show you in third place with 20 percent of the vote. The incumbent has 35 percent and in second place is a millionaire candidate with 26 percent. You have under $40,000 to spend. What do you do?

This was the question for the Carol Moseley Braun for Senate campaign in Illinois during the senatorial primary in 1992.

Braun was the Cook County Clerk, and a former state representative. I met her during the 1988 Jackson campaign. She called to ask me to run her campaign. I politely declined but volunteered to help her get started.

Alan Dixon, a.k.a. "Al the pal," was a two-term incumbent who had never been beaten dating back to his days as a local elected official. He made a very costly mistake. In 1991 he voted to confirm Clarence Thomas to the Supreme Court. His vote to confirm Thomas certainly raised the ire of Democratic women voters, but it also raised the question of how he could vote to confirm Thomas when he voted against Robert Bork for the Supreme Court. Most would argue that Bork at least was qualified and Thomas was not.

Al Hofeld was a multimillionaire who was convinced by his consultant David Axelrod that if he spent $2 million he could upset Dixon. He began spending on TV six months before the primary. Dixon answered. For a few months, you could not turn on the television without seeing a Dixon or Hofeld spot. Carol just stayed back and watched. Who knew that the voters would become tired of the negative ads of the two leading candidates?

After my negative response to her invitation to run the campaign, she hired Kozie Matthews as campaign manager. Kozie was an aide to Jackson during the 1988 campaign. He called and asked if I would come on board as a consultant to the campaign, saying he did not know anything about running a campaign and needed my help. In addition, I could do the media if they ever had any money.

Carol had confided in me that she was really a protest candidate with no real chance of winning. She called me and told me that Al Hofeld had entered the race and asked what I thought it meant. I responded, "Now you can win." In a three-way race, she needed less than 40 percent to win.

But Carol could not get the press to pay attention to her campaign. She was viewed as a protest candidate, and one with no money to boot.

One day, I noticed an item in the paper announcing that Senator George Mitchell, the Senate Majority Leader would be appearing with Senator Dixon in Chicago at a press conference on healthcare. I encouraged Carol to attend the news conference. She thought that would be impolite. I responded that Mitchell was coming to Chicago to help his friend and colleague who knew very little about healthcare. The press conference would feature a photo op of the two senators and would be dominated by Mitchell with a well-crafted quote from Dixon. I told Carol that we would go and stand in the back of the room. The press would notice we were there but we would not interrupt the press conference. At the end of the conference, we would hand out a release detailing Braun's platform on healthcare. She would answer the reporters' questions and blow them away with her knowledge of the subject. And that is exactly what happened.

The main benefit to Carol was the she had won over the press. She now was considered viable, although still a long shot.

I advised that we go on the air. With very little money to purchase time and even less to produce an ad, I devised an idea that would at best be a crapshoot. We pull all of our limited resources in Chicago TV, except for a mailing to single women, head of household in the Chicago suburbs. This mailing would emphasize why women should vote for Carol.

The TV ad was done very cheaply ($1,008) and very quickly. Instead of using footage which we could not afford, I used still photos.

A picture of Dixon appeared. The voice over said, "This is Alan Dixon. He's a lawyer and a millionaire and he wants to be reelected. He thinks he owns the seat." The word *own* appears in green letters under his name. Next a picture of Hofeld appeared. The voice over said, "This is Al Hofeld. He's a lawyer and a millionaire and he wants to buy the seat." The word *buy* appears under his name.

Then a picture of Carol appears between the pics of Dixon and Hofeld. The voice over said, "This is Carol Moseley Braun. She's a mother and she wants to earn the seat." The word *earn* appears under her name. The other two pics disappear with the picture of Carol remaining. The voice-over said "Vote for Carol Moseley Braun. She's not a millionaire and she wants to earn your vote." We previewed the spot for the press which ensured the ad would run on TV for free as part of the news.

On election day, Carol was at the beauty parlor when she received a phone call informing her that the afternoon exit polls were very encouraging. Later that night, she received 38 percent to Dixon's 35 percent and Hofeld's 27 percent. Dixon, in one of the classiest acts of political history, quickly conceded and pledged to help Carol with the fall race.

Carol's victory was the number one story in the world. I told Kozie to have Carol greet commuters the next morning at Union Station. Her appearance was covered live and rebroadcast throughout the day.

Carol was in demand. Washington, DC, called. The Black Caucus wanted to meet her. Senator Mitchell wanted to meet with her and arrange for the Democratic

Senatorial Campaign Committee to do all they could to ensure her victory. Women's groups like EMILY'S List, who gave her a $500 contribution during the primary, were claiming their help was the difference in her election victory.

We scheduled a trip to the nation's capital. Gary LaPaille, the state Democratic Party chairman, who tried to talk Carol out of running, appeared uninvited in Washington. He had rented a limo to transport Carol around the city. I advised her not to ride in the limo. It was a bad impression to convey. She reluctantly agreed.

We arrived at our first appointment with Senator Bill Bradley a few minutes late. Bradley was in the hall outside of his office and nervously pacing.

Bradley had been asked to campaign for Dixon but declined. He was an old friend of Carol's. Although he could not openly help her, he could conveniently be unable to help Dixon. Bradley greeted Carol with a hug. We entered his office and his staff was lined up and started applauding when they caught sight of Carol. Most of the women staffers were in tears. They grabbed her hand and hugged her.

While this was taking place, I was staring at a picture on the Senator's wall. He was in the arms of Willis Reed. It was during the 1970 basketball championship game. Bradley came over and I told him I was a lifelong Knicks fan and was so emotional during that game that I cried when they won. He told me that Willis was telling him to sit down because the game was not over yet.

Next we visited Senator Mitchell. I thanked him for helping us win. He looked puzzled. I reminded him of the healthcare news conference and how it actually helped our campaign. He smiled and said, "You deserved to win."

After leaving Mitchell on our way across to the House side of the Capitol, we were stopped by two Capital guards—an African American male and a white female. They both had tears in their eyes as they shook Carol's hand and told her how much her victory meant to them.

Carol realized the historic magnitude of the victory she had won.

Nothing Succeeds as Planned

J. Warren Tompkins

My breakthrough in politics happened in 1978, when I was volunteering for Strom Thurmond's senatorial campaign. I eventually worked my way up to "statewide coordinator of special events." After that election, Lee Atwater, who was a childhood friend, Carroll Campbell, a first-term member of Congress, and I went to work for Ronald Reagan in the South Carolina primary. Reagan won the 1980 primary, with the endorsement of Senator Thurmond, and went on to the White House. Reagan's coattails helped elect a Republican majority in the U.S. Senate for the first time in many years.

Harry Dent, who was credited with getting President Richard Nixon reelected in 1972 through his "Southern Strategy," convinced Atwater he should go to the White House to be in the political shop. Harry then tells Strom, "you need a guy in the White House political operation, like I was in the old days with Nixon."

Then Harry says to Strom, Lee, and Carroll, "Look, when I went to Washington, I didn't leave anybody behind to take care of home base for me. Y'all need to find somebody to cover your backside in South Carolina."

Campbell wanted me to go to Congress with him to be his administrative assistant, which I seriously wanted to do. But they told me, "We need you to stay home and run the Republican Party for a few years, until we figure out what to do next."

I figured what the heck, at least I would be a big fish somewhere. So I go to work for the state Republican Party and when I got in there I found out that the party was broke. We had a $110,000 deficit and our operating costs were $140,000. I had a great chairman and we had a lot of help, but the whole thing was a mess.

Back in 1978 Thurmond had said, "This is my last election," so Campbell was gearing up for to run for Thurmond's senate seat in 1984. But when the Republicans took control of the U.S. Senate in 1980, everything changed.

Thurmond decides, "I've got all this responsibility and it would be a disservice on my part to walk away now that we have all this power in Washington. I said I was done, but if the people want me to run again, I will." And he runs again for re-election to the senate.

All of a sudden, Campbell's plans to run for the Senate are out the window. So we are scrambling around trying to figure out what to do and Strom says, "Democrats are going to have a weak field statewide. We need to talk Campbell in to running for governor." And so we did—in 1986.

The hard sell though was Campbell's wife because she was all comfortable with her new congressional life. She had a job working at a department store and was having a nice time doing all this socializing in Washington, DC. We had to convince her that it would be great to come back to be South Carolina's First Lady.

We started planning the details of how and where we were going to make the announcement for governor.

The entire campaign staff flies out to this little town in South Carolina with two of our most trusted party helpers. They were older guys—it's not like we had eighteen-year-old guys or anything. They went out and got this brand-spanking-new van and it was just all shiny and everything. We all pile into the van and we head into downtown for the press conference. We get out on the highway going into town and the van starts shaking and suddenly it just dies.

They had done everything but get gas.

So here we are, stuck out on the highway trying to flag down anybody and every-body to give us a ride so we don't miss our first press conference.

Lo and behold this young couple that looked like remnants from the Vietnam War protests drive up in this big old van. It wasn't a Volkswagen van but it was painted red and inside it had shag carpet on the floors, with a big old lazy boy chair in the back.

They were kind enough to stop and offer to take us into town. We had to pull Campbell into the van, kicking and screaming. "No, my career is over. It's over. I can't pull up to the press conference in this. What are people going to say?"

I said, "Well, this *is* going to make the news. *The front page of the news.*"

Campbell's wife was so mortified when she got into the van that she didn't want to sit down or touch anything. She thought she was going to catch some kind of bug.

So we all pull up to that press conference in that run-down hippie van.

We actually got a great story out of it. We went from thinking that the world was over to this-really-didn't-hurt-us-at-all because we made a big thing about how good these people were, how helpful they had been, and their willingness to give us a ride.

The campaign was nearly over before it started because we almost didn't make it to that first press conference to announce our candidacy.

We ended up winning that campaign by 25,000 votes.

I Ran for Team Mascot

Steve Cohen

My first real involvement in campaigning was when I attended Vanderbilt. It was 1969 and I decided to run for a student government office. At the time I really wanted to go work for John Jay Hooker, a rising politician, described as the "Kennedy" of Tennessee, on his 1970 campaign for governor. But I had limited experience when it came to campaigns and I didn't know Hooker personally.

So I ran for "Mr. Commodore." Mr. Commodore was one of only two student body-wide elected positions in the school: one position was Student Government Association President and the other was Mr. Commodore.

Mr. Commodore represents the civic school spirit. It's really the mascot for the basketball and football teams, although in those days you didn't have to wear a paper-mache head and feet. You greeted the basketball players from both schools when they were introduced, shook their hands, and welcomed the other team. You lead the cheers at all basketball and football games.

I wanted to be Mr. Commodore in my upcoming junior year, which meant running as a sophomore. There was no rule you had to be a senior, but seniors apparently had always served in the position of Mr. Commodore. All three of my opponents would be running as juniors and take office as seniors if they won.

I figured that I had a base in my sophomore class, since my three opponents were all juniors, and that the freshmen wouldn't have a candidate, so I could build a base there.

I went door-to-door in the freshman dorm and asked people to vote. The first election ended in a runoff because nobody got a majority; I was ahead by six votes.

In the runoff election, I won by two votes. I worked up at the C room, which was the dining hall. I shook hands with everyone who came in the hall, shook hands with everyone who came out to vote, and shook hands with people who supported me. My opponent, instead of campaigning, spent his time playing pool in the Beta house.

I always thought I was smarter than him. I knew how to work the voting precincts and shake hands, which is probably how I won by two votes.

In a small turnout election, as you well know, getting a large turnout from your base is sometimes enough to win. Maybe by playing pool in the Beta house, he got forty Beta guys, or even sixty or eighty Beta guys to vote for him. Maybe that was *his* game plan. *But I won.*

In 1969 our first football game that year was an away game at Michigan. Turns out they weren't taking the cheerleaders to Michigan because there wasn't room for them on the plane. I got on the phone and called around and got three different wealthy alums to agree to fly some of the cheerleaders to the Michigan game. I also put a story out in the paper, "Mr. Commodore looking for airplanes, looking for help."

John Jay Hooker was one of the people who responded to my appeal. In fact, I flew to the Michigan game in John Jay's plane. During the flight I asked him if he would give me a job working for his campaign. And he said yes.

So I was going to work for John Jay Hooker that next summer, in 1970, just as I had hoped. Then I had an opportunity to work for a company in Ohio in a trainee program in the summer. I thought about doing that but decided to turn it down to stay home and work for Hooker for governor.

Then sometime around May, I got a call from Aaron Wyckoff, who was with the Hooker campaign. He said, "Steve, there's no job. The candidate *has* to say yes, but there's no job."

I was caught off guard, "But John Jay Hooker said there was a job."

He said, "The candidate *has* to say yes, but he can't. I'm telling you *that's* what he *has* to say, *but there is no job.*"

I figure I've been screwed. I gave up a summer trainee job and now I didn't have a job with Hooker. So I got out the Tennessee Blue Book and saw that in my district, no Democrat had run for Statehouse in 1968 because it had become so Republican.

I found out that if you got the requisite number of signatures, which was twenty-five, you're the nominee. And I thought, *if I can't work for a candidate*, I'll *be* a candidate. I went door-to-door and got the twenty-five signatures I needed and became the Democratic nominee for Statehouse in 1970.

I also ran the youth campaign for Hooker's primary opponent in Shelby County, Stan Snodgrass. I decided screw Hooker, and went to work for Snodgrass, worked for that campaign while I was running as the Democratic nominee for the Statehouse.

I lost my race in the general election but led the ticket in the district; I got more Democratic votes, percentage-wise, than anyone else.

In the general election John Jay Hooker was running against Republican Winfield Dunn, who lived in my district. Hooker lost and Dunn became the first Republican in fifty years to win the governorship. Hooker ran for statewide office numerous times but never won a general election.

I was elected to the Tennessee Senate in 1982 where I served for twenty-four years. In 2006 I was elected to Congress where I'm currently serving my fifth term.

I still shake a lot of hands. . . .

Advancing in Nebraska

John Rendon

At one point during the George McGovern presidential campaign in 1972, I get sent to Nebraska in advance of the candidate's visit.

I learned everything I needed to know about the Platte River. I remember driving out to Scottsbluff. We were planning a whistle-stop train tour just like the one Bobby Kennedy did and Scottsbluff was going to be the farthest stop.

I drove the whole route and checked out all the train stations. Then I circled back around to go to Hastings, Nebraska. I'm listening to the radio and there is a tornado warning. It suddenly occurs to me that I am in a tornado state.

I look around and those clouds aren't grey but green. I'm thinking "holy sh*t." And sure enough off in the distance there was a tornado on the ground. This Chrysler I'm driving got up to about 160 mph and I lit out of there. I left the tornado in the background.

I went to Hastings to see a farm run by a guy named Glenn Burke who was with McGovern on farms, but conservative on other issues. He thought that someone should be president who knows what farmers go through.

We also planned on doing an event in Hastings with veterans. As I recall, it was a veteran-owned business where they made plastic piping for irrigation. They had two product lines but they could expand to four. It was a question of the federal government creating a better loan environment so this expansion could happen.

I go in and do a tour of the facility and figure out the best camera angles. This is when advance teams were just one person, not five or ten the way they are in campaigns today.

Everything's in place and the plane lands at Hastings, where I meet up with the candidate and traveling staff. I brief them on the event on the way to the location. But when we get to the factory there is nobody there. I said, "Why is there nobody here? I mean I left here an hour ago and there were fifteen people ready for the tour."

The guy said, "I'm really sorry but we had a problem. Something erupted on our production line and rather than embarrass Senator McGovern, I sent everyone home." I thought: great—thanks a lot.

So I quickly improvised a tour and showed them what the line would have looked like if workers were there!

After the tour I called Glenn Burke up and said, "Are you ready for a visit from the man running for President of the United States?"

I remembered telling McGovern that we were going to look at the irrigation pipes and then go to a farm to talk to a farmer. So we rescued the stop from a total catastrophe.

I'm confident that because of the dynamic of ubiquitous transparency and the platform of social media, rescues and recoveries like this one may no longer be possible.

Sometimes You Get Lucky

Dale Emmons

Early one morning in late April of 1999, I received a call from a familiar Kentucky mountain voice. It was from my long-time political friend Denzil Ray Hall. Denzil is from Floyd County in the mountains of Eastern Kentucky. Denzil had worked for former Kentucky Senator Walter "Dee" Huddleston. Denzil's son, Doug Hall, was also the elected Circuit Court Clerk in Floyd County.

Denzil says, "Dale, we need your help. My niece Connie Hancock was recently appointed by Governor Patton to be Property Valuation Administrator (PVA) here in Floyd County. As you may know, my brother Lovell Hall died while holding the office and Connie is his stepdaughter. She worked for Lovell in his office for several years. We had the Governor appoint her to succeed Lovell. And now she's campaigning to keep her job.

"We have a problem. It's complicated, and we really need to talk to you to see if you can help us. We can't talk about this on the phone. Would you mind meeting Connie and me at Natural Bridge State Park later today?"

So I agreed to meet them at five o'clock at Natural Bridge State Park. This is sixty miles from my office. I did not know and had never met Connie Hancock and really had no clue what this was all about. Denzil met me in the lobby of the park's Hemlock Lodge. He took me into the restaurant and introduced me to his niece.

"Dale, this is Connie. I know I can trust you and I have told Connie she can trust you too. She's, uh, got herself in a tight spot here. We'll explain why in a moment. Are you familiar with Glenn David May who is the son of—"

I interrupt him saying, "I know who Glenn David May is. He's married to Judge James Allen's daughter, Allison May. I know the whole family, his mother Louise— know 'em all—his father is David May who owns May Truck Body." The parents were well-known successful business people.

He continues with his lead-in on why I'm here. "Well, Glenn David is running against Connie in the May primary. My guess is that he has probably already spent more than a $100,000." This was a big sum for the job as local tax assessor in Floyd County. This is a job that probably pays a little more than $50,000 a year. "Dale we can scrape up about $40,000 to spend. If you can find a way for her to win, we'll find another $5,000 as a bonus for you. You can spend what we got, but we'll give you that $5,000 if you find a way for her to win. I am afraid she is gonna get beat if we don't do something different."

"Now I'm gonna leave and let Connie here explain to you what's goin' on. She may not wanna say some of this stuff in front of me. I don't wanta...well, I want to make sure she can tell you herself. Now Connie here knows she can trust you...so, I'm gonna let you two talk."

Denzil left and I turned and addressed Connie, "What's going on Connie?"

In a familiar and typical mountain accent she says, "Glenn David May is trying to destroy my family to win this election. He has a videotape he's been showin' everybody. He has been sayin' I had an affair with somebody. He is telling people that because of this, I am not fit and shouldn't be elected PVA."

She paused and then continued, "He's sent people to threaten me. He is saying that if I talk about his family in any way, that he will put this video on TV." She then hands me an envelope containing a VHS videotape. I was puzzled because I knew the May family. They are well-known and well-respected; I had no idea what it could be that they were this concerned about.

I asked Connie what was on the tape. She explained in detail! I thought for a moment and asked her if she thought he would really do what he said he would do? "Yeah, I think he will."

I asked her, "How will you, your husband, and your two teenage daughters feel if he were to put the tape on TV?" Having heard a description of the tape's contents, I wasn't certain the local TV station would even air a commercial containing the material described.

Her answer was firm, "At this point it doesn't really matter, he's been going around showing it to everybody already. My husband knows about it. My daughters know about it."

I wasn't certain what I was going to do but my read on Connie Hancock was good. She was ready and willing to fight. I thought she was being bullied. I liked her and just needed her assurance that she would allow me free rein on managing whatever message we came up with. She was willing to let me run the campaign and to follow my directions for the time remaining until election day.

She said, "Yes sir, I am all in."

So I agreed to help with her campaign. The word gets out that I had been hired. In a couple of days I received a phone call from Jerry Patton, who was helping the opponent with his campaign. Jerry is an experienced political operative, a former commonwealth's attorney and local lawyer. He had been in the Young Democrats with us, so I knew him. He says, "Now Dale if you or Connie's campaign uses the dispute over Glenn David May's family's delinquent property taxes against him then he is gonna put that tape on TV."

I said, "Jerry, do you really think he would do that?"

He responded that he did. I expressed my appreciation for his calling me to give me a heads up. I really did appreciate the call. I learned from that call that Glenn David May would use the tape and that his family's tax issue was the sensitive subject. The latter was something I did not know before his call.

I immediately called Connie and told her, "Connie, we're gonna win this race."

For context, it is important to note that this was after the Republican Congress had impeached Bill Clinton over the Monica Lewinsky affair. We were in a Democratic primary where under Kentucky law Republicans couldn't vote. My bet was that Democrats were already incensed about what the Republicans had done to Clinton. The plan was to set a trap for this guy; a trigger to allow him to fulfill his threat. We did the necessary opposition research to get the details on the unpaid property taxes. We wanted them to know we were coming!

Sometimes you get lucky in politics. I got lucky. I had a young woman working for me at the time by the name of Amanda Durbin. Amanda told me that she had heard of Glenn David May. She said that she thought he had been in some kind of trouble while he was a student at Eastern Kentucky University. EKU is located where I live and work.

So I directed Amanda to go to the Richmond Police Department to do an open records request on Glenn David May. We hit paydirt. The request yielded a three-inch-thick stack of papers. In final analysis, Mr. May had been arrested and charged with violations of the law fifty-six times while he had been a student at Eastern Kentucky University.

We produced what I would describe as a "monster truck commercial," both in style and because I hired this Houston, Texas, voice talent that does many of the monster truck commercials seen on TV. The guy had this big booming voice.

The narrative of the trigger ad went something like this, "If you elect Glenn David May, Floyd County will really pay. His wealthy family had to be sued for not paying their property taxes." Copies of their delinquent tax bills and a copy of the lawsuit were put on the screen as validation.

Our production budget was tight. We found some inexpensive old silent movie stock footage. They were black and white video clips. One was of two men fighting and choking each other and another of cops throwing a convict into jail. The voice-over says, "He has been charged with violating the law fifty-six times. In a drunken brawl he even bit a man's ear completely off." To add some more humor, our video editor added a nice touch. A set of comic false teeth chopping through the corner of the frame!

We put that ad up on Thursday night with a plan to change traffic the next day. It was scheduled to come down Friday night, at the last possible minute, to alter traffic going into the week before the election. Our gamble was they would go up with their response ad of the sex tape on Friday. They did not disappoint us. Their ad went up on Friday night.

Our ad switched and went positive airing an ad with Connie Hancock speaking to the camera with her husband standing by her. "Anyone who wants power this bad shouldn't be trusted in office," Connie said. Her husband added, "We want every fair and decent-minded voter to stand with us."

May's ad was not well received. We were fortunate that the TV station ran the May spot so folks would understand our rebuttal. Once the response was known, which was immediately, it was too late for May to pull his ad down. The ad continued to air with a heavy schedule throughout the weekend. The nature of the attack spot was so personal and so ugly that I am told that Glenn David May couldn't go out in public. His friends were even disgusted. Connie became the heroine by remaining positive even as she was being smeared.

The tape they had was the cheesiest, most awful thing you've ever seen, and the ad made national news. It starts with Glenn David May, who looks like a teenage kid, standing there holding this video tape in his hand. He says, "My opponent is attacking me because she doesn't want you to see this tape. She's been unfaithful to her husband."

All I could think was "I can't believe this sucker is doing this."

Then this grainy footage starts of this woman taking all of her clothes off and sitting down on the bed. Connie Hancock had a very unique hair style, and the woman in the footage looked something like Connie. The video was extremely poor quality; there no way to identify who was on the tape.

I had anticipated that reporters were going to ask whether this was Connie in the tape. I had decided to decline to answer this direct question. Instead Connie would respond through a written statement, "I never allowed *anyone* to make a video of my husband and I having sex." That is all that we gave them, so that is all they had!

The story shows up on CBS, ABC, NBC, and CNN; the Kentucky press goes crazy. It was a feeding frenzy.

In anticipation, I had called Ron Faucheux, then the editor and publisher of *Campaign & Elections* magazine. After having discussed the dynamics of what was playing out, I decided to refer reporters to Ron.

Their question to Ron was, "have you ever heard of anyone putting a video clip of a naked woman in a campaign ad?"

His answer was, "Nah, *I never heard of anything like that.*" So that became the story line: no one had ever done this kind of sleazy ad before. Here this guy running for tax assessor in Floyd County, Kentucky, is running this despicable ad that really crosses the line and you can't even tell who is on the tape.

Needless to say, Connie won. The best revenge is always winning big.

To make the story even better, Glenn David May's father-in-law, Judge James Allen, the district court judge, had drawn an opponent in the general election. He had not been opposed in the primary.

A month or so later I receive a phone call. Judge Allen, who was a star football player at the University of Kentucky, has a big deep voice. On the phone he says, "Mr. Emmons, this is Judge James Allen from Prestonsburg, Kentucky. I was calling to inquire as to whether you might be available for consultation."

Stunned, I said, "Well, Judge, before I answer that question, you need to know who I am."

He said, "Aww, I know who you are, that's why I'm calling. I still want you to come see me. We want to hire you to help me in this campaign."

I helped defeat his son-in-law and now he is hiring me to run his race! My appearance at his fundraiser later that month was like being part of a cattle show. He brings me into town for this fundraiser to show everyone who he has in his corner.

My recollection is that I was paid $10,000 to sign on with his campaign, *and this was for a district judge race in Floyd County, Kentucky.* The funny thing about this business of politics is you just never know what is around the next corner.

Connie Hancock is still the PVA in Floyd County. She has not drawn an opponent since her initial primary win.

II. Political Communication

You Have to Ask for Every Vote

Nancy Korman

One of Speaker Tip O'Neill's favorite stories, when he visited classrooms, was about his next door neighbor, an elderly woman who lived alone.

Every time there was a snowstorm Tip would go over and shovel her walkway. After one election day, Tip asked her, "Did you vote for me?"

She said, "No, Tip I didn't." So he said, "Why not?" And she responded, "Because you never asked me."

Tip said, "I never forgot that. Always remember, you have to ask for every vote."

When Attacked, You Have to Respond

Bob Mulholland

On April 11, 1996, the *Washington Times* breaks a news story about Democratic National Committee officials attacking President Bill Clinton about his marriage.

I went online and made the statement, "If they are attacking Bill Clinton, let's look at the divorce rate of the House Judiciary Committee members."

As a result of my comments four House Members, including a woman from Idaho, got exposed by the local press. Republican Henry Hyde was also exposed for having extramarital affairs.

I knew from my experience in Vietnam, when attacked, you have to respond to the attack. In the last three decades, I think Democrats have become very timid and weak communicators.

Take the case, for example, of the Christmas bombing in 2009—the suspect had gotten a visa under President Bush. But every Republican commentator on TV was attacking the hell out of President Obama. The Democrats were on the defensive and this made the public think: "why did the Obama administration give this guy a visa?"

Not responding to the attack was a mistake.

A Powerful Message

Rich Schlackman

While working for Tom Hayden and Jane Fonda's Campaign for Economic Development (CED), I was sent to Santa Monica to work field on a state assembly race. I had five hundred volunteers.

I often had to build a crowd for events in the San Francisco area. I had two groups I could rely on to show up for events: Delancey Street, which was a nonprofit that helps substance abusers, ex-convicts, homeless, and others who have hit rock bottom, and the People's Temple, run by Reverend Jim Jones.

The same people would show up for each event. We asked them to wear different clothes, so the reporters would concentrate on the diversity of the crowd, instead of noticing it was always the same people.

Our opponent was doing direct mail, so whenever they did a mailing, I crank out the mimeo machine and send my volunteers out with a response. We lost the election, mainly because we did not do mail.

Tom and Jane decided, since I liked working with numbers, that I would be their mail guy. That's how I got involved in the direct mail business.

I had never done a piece of mail in my life. I couldn't even draw a straight line with a ruler. I went back to San Francisco and decided I needed to learn how to do mail. But there was no teacher. I had to learn about computers, design and content on my own.

I started doing direct mail for the Democratic Congressional Campaign Committee (DCCC) when Congressman Vic Fazio was the chairman. One of the races I did was against a Republican congressman.

Every week, our opponent would publish and mail a pseudo-newspaper—highlighted by an important issue of the week. Vic called me and said, "Do something about this." So I did a mailing.

What I learned from doing that direct mail piece was the need to respond when your opponent does mail. Never let any mailing go unanswered.

I was fortunate to learn a lot from Tony Schwartz, who was the best message framer—*ever*. He taught me that the greatest emotion is "shame."

"*Shame on You*" is a very powerful message. I incorporated Tony's teachings into my work from that point on.

Texas Swagger in Vermont

Paul Curcio

In 1992, I was the political director of the National Republican Senatorial Committee and worked for the new committee chairman, Senator Phil Gramm of Texas.

I had become obsessed with defeating Senator Patrick Leahy in Vermont. Gramm didn't particularly care for Leahy but we couldn't find a Republican candidate to run against him. All of a sudden, in the middle of the 1992 election cycle, the Vermont secretary of state becomes a possibility.

He's sort of a typical New England character—his name is Jim Douglas—who went on to be the governor for many terms. But this was way before that, when he was just secretary of state. I think he had been elected like three times, every two years, so he had a presence in the state—they knew him.

So he comes down to Washington, DC, and I'm thinking, "Bingo. This is the guy. This guy is perfect. He's perfect for New England." He's on the moderate side of the ideological spectrum—he's a little "gosh, golly, gee"—perfect! His demeanor was just right.

So I call Phil Gramm on the phone and I said, "Senator, we've got our candidate in Vermont."

A few months later we're making progress with the campaign and we arrange to do a fundraiser up in Burlington with Gramm as the speaker.

My antenna goes way up because I didn't think Gramm's Texas swagger and style—that I'd come to love so much and still do—was going to sell in Vermont. So I had to tamp him down, but there is only so much you can do to tamp Phil Gramm down.

So I took it upon myself, rather than one of the field guys, to write the briefing paper.

I put together a briefing paper that gave him the key points—what he should say, what he shouldn't say, polling data, and so forth. Well I think I'm starting to make progress and I stress to him over and over in this memorandum, "You have to understand that these people are not like us. These people up there are not like us. To your eyes it's going to look like socialism. You have to temper your remarks."

I send it over to him and he goes up to do the event. He's in the car, driving back to the airport after the event and he calls me and says, "Paul, listen." He would always say that.

"Paul, listen, I just came out of this event in Burlington. I don't know what you're talking about—all this socialism up here—I didn't see any of it."

I said, "What do you mean?" He says, "I walked into that place and I was like a rock star. I showed up and I gave my usual talk like I do in Texas and I had them up out of their chairs clapping and screaming—*it was unbelievable. I think I could get elected up here.*"

"Senator how many people were in that room?" He said, "Three hundred and fifty." And I said, "That's the total number of votes you'd get if you ran up there."

That was not what he wanted to hear.

So I repeated, "Those are the only votes you would get—at that fundraiser you saw every vote you would get in the state with that message. OK?"

The two of us were just talking past each other when it came to Vermont.

The Farmer Ad

Jerry Austin

During the Democratic Iowa caucuses of 1988, I convinced Jesse Jackson that he needed to be on television. Television was one of the measurements used by the press to define a viable candidate.

In his 1984 attempt to win the Democratic Party presidential nomination, Jackson's only paid media was $10,000 for radio in Los Angeles. It was important, I argued, that we be on the air during the caucuses, not only to win more votes but also to establish viability with the press corps.

I wrote an ad for Jackson to deliver to the camera and booked a studio to record and edit. Jackson was not feeling well that day. His performance was mediocre. We did a number of takes and I was satisfied that I could develop a spot from the footage we shot.

In the edit suite, I realized I could not air any of this material. Not only did Jackson not look good because of his illness, he sounded even worse. I realized Jackson's forte was talking to an audience for an hour, not a camera for thirty seconds. His communications acumen was to bring an audience to a crescendo, which was impossible in thirty seconds. I decided not to put him on the air.

The reason to be on the air in Iowa was still valid but I needed a different ad. I returned to my Chicago office to ponder what to do. I was under the gun. We had bought media time that would begin in forty-eight hours and I did not have a spot to send the stations.

I noticed a VHS tape on my desk. I had never seen this tape before. I was told it was the footage from Jackson's announcement in October which included footage from Raleigh, North Carolina, and Des Moines, Iowa. I found a VCR player and viewed the footage. I could not believe my eyes.

In the footage of Iowa, there was a scene in a tent where two large farmers were standing at a podium before an audience of Jackson supporters. Jackson and his wife were seated to the side of the podium. One of the farmers told the story of how Jackson had helped save his farm by interceding with the bank. He gives Jesse credit for saving his farm and why it was important to elect Jackson President.

I immediately realized that with a bit of editing, I had the spot I wanted. Here were two white men saying it was ok to support a black man for President and using his help on their behalf as validation.

I edited the tape. I did not use a voice over. I played the tape in Iowa. On caucus day, Jackson received 10 percent of the vote, a 1000 percent increase over his 1 percent in 1984. We may have finished behind rival Dick Gephardt, Mike Dukakis, and Paul Simon, but we could justifiably claim that we had won because of the comparison to 1984. And everyone was talking about the farmer ad.

The farmer ad soon became our one and only ad. Wherever we were campaigning, the farmer ad would air. The ad never mentioned that the footage was shot in Iowa. In each state in which the spot aired, the voters believed the two farmers were from their state.

Actually, the farmers were from Missouri. They had traveled to Iowa on their own to thank Jesse for his help. They were added to the program at the last minute. The farmer spot helped us finish in almost a dead heat in Kansas and Montana and a tie for first in the twenty primaries held on Super Tuesday.

After the campaign, the American Association of Political Consultants awarded me a "Pollie" for the farmer spot.

Always Go with Your Instincts

Jerry Austin

During the 1988 New York Democratic primary, I was introduced to Spike Lee. Spike was becoming a well-known filmmaker, but he was not as famous then as he would become.

We met at Sylvia's, the famous soul food restaurant in Harlem. Spike was wearing his Yankee hat and appeared even shorter than I had envisioned.

He told me he wanted to produce and direct a television ad for Reverend Jesse Jackson. Reverend Jackson had blessed the set of his last movie and he wanted to help in the campaign. He wanted the spot to be about drugs. He believed that white people would vote for Jackson if they knew how tough he was on drug users and pushers.

He asked me to write the spot and call him when it was completed.

As I traveled back downtown, I thought to myself of the lesson I learned in Iowa. Jackson is not good in thirty-second spots. His forte is to speak to thousands of people for a half an hour or more; his speech would bring people to a crescendo. The TV spot I produced in Iowa never was aired because Jesse was too uptight. But this was Spike Lee, not Jerry Austin.

I returned to my hotel room and wrote the spot. Spike and his cameraman Ernest Dickerson, who would attain fame in his own right, came to my hotel room to go over the script and plan the shoot.

They liked my script, especially since it had both suburban and inner-city settings. Drugs were permeating all neighborhoods, not just the ghetto.

The highlight of the shoot was filming on a crack street in Harlem. We failed to alert the Secret Service to our schedule. They were mad and rightly so. We kept the press away, shooting the spot during the daily time reporters use to file their stories.

As he exited the car, Jackson was greeted with cheers and screams. As Jackson went inside a small building to have makeup applied, Spike addressed the crowd that was starting to gather using a bullhorn.

He explained that we were there to shoot a television commercial for Reverend Jackson. He asked for their help. When he yelled quiet, he wanted all noise to cease. He asked if they could do that and the crowd either nodded or shouted yes.

When Jackson returned to the street, he was wearing a flak jacket under his shirt. The Secret Service insisted he wear the jacket for protection. Normally, when any form of filming is done in New York, you obtain a permit and also the help of the New York Police Department. We did not seek a permit, but we did have a few beat cops at the shoot.

After dozens of takes, Spike was happy and Jackson departed for his next event.

I accompanied Spike and his crew back to Brooklyn to his studio/editing suite. The studio was in an apartment building in Fort Greene. I had not been to Fort Greene since I was a caseworker for the New York City Department of Welfare ten years earlier. As I looked around Spike's studio, I felt like I had been there before. Spike informed me that this apartment/studio was the main setting of his first film "She's Gotta Have It." After a few hours the spot was finished and ready to be delivered to the television stations.

In anticipation of the subject matter and the importance of the New York primary, I purchased $700,000 of New York television time. You could not turn on the TV without seeing this spot.

After two days, Jackson reported that he was getting a very negative reaction to the spot. The criticism was that Jackson was scaring people. He looked so big on screen and his demeanor was so serious it was crazy. I pulled the spot.

Spike called the next day and asked what reaction the spot had evoked. I told him I pulled the spot because it scared people. He was shocked.

Then I told him my story about Iowa and he asked why I did not share that experience with him. I responded that he was Spike Lee, perhaps he would be more successful than I was.

He laughed and said: always go with your instincts.

An Obvious Endorser

Jerry Austin

During the 1988 Jackson presidential campaign, it was not unusual to be summoned to Jackson's South Side home for an impromptu staff meeting.

I walked in to the house and heard Jackson call for me to come into the kitchen. I walked in and he handed me the phone ordering, "Talk to Bill." I said hello thinking it was one of our staff, Bill Morton. It was not Bill Morton, but Bill Cosby.

Mr. Cosby asked, "What can I do to help the campaign?" I answered, "I have two requests. One is to do a benefit concert for the campaign in Iowa and second is to appear in a television ad." His response was an immediate "yes" to both. He told me to write the copy for the ad and send it to him in New York. I would be called and told when the spot would be filmed. It would take place on a Thursday immediately after taping his number-one television sitcom.

Finding entertainers to do benefit concerts for the campaign was not a problem. The problem was keeping the cost down. Singers need a band. Stevie Wonder would appear anywhere we wanted but he had to have his band. Bill Cosby needed a stool. Cosby eventually performed at a concert at the University of Iowa that was mildly successful.

I wrote the script for the television ad and sent it to New York. Within a few days, I was told the ad would be filmed the next Thursday. I flew in to New York from Chicago and took a cab to the NBC studios in Queens.

I was expected and ushered to a seat in the studio audience. I was told the taping of the spot would start after the show finished taping.

There were two bleachers full of spectators. In between scenes, the audience was kept laughing by two stand-up comics who "worked the crowd."

After the taping was completed, I was escorted on to the set and introduced to Mr. Cosby. He shook my hand and informed me that he would not be using my script. Before I could respond and ask why, he walked toward a sofa chair in the living room set and sat down. He asked, "How many seconds do I have?" I answered, "26.5."

He lowered his head then looked up and said, "ready." A voice from an unseen control booth called out, "action." Cosby started talking. "Sometimes there's someone you want to vote for, but you don't think they can win, so you vote for someone else. Make a change in yourself. Vote for someone you really believe in." He stopped and the control voice called out "26.5." One take on the nose.

Then Cosby instructed me, "Make sure you have a voice-over say, 'Vote for Jesse Jackson for President.'" He stood up, shook my hand, and left.

One of his staffers escorted me out to the lobby and I was asked to wait a few minutes for the tape to be delivered to me. After receiving the tape, I spent the night at a hotel at La Guardia Airport before boarding a plane for Columbus, Ohio, the next morning. I would be posting the ad at The Media Group, a firm I had been using for ten years.

We were very excited. Bill Cosby was then the number one entertainer in the world and we would be editing a spot featuring him in support of Jesse Jackson. We entered the edit suite and put the tape in the VCR. It was blank. We fast forwarded, rewound, and it was still blank. I called Cosby's producer in New York and told her about the blank tape. She placed me on hold and when she returned she had found the right tape and promised to Fed Ex it for next day delivery.

The next day it arrived and we returned to the edit suite to complete the thirty-second ad. The tape was fine, but we noticed that during Cosby's 26.5 seconds to the camera, he did not mention Jackson's name. No problem, I thought, we would cut away from Cosby, show some footage of Jackson and return to Cosby. As the screen went to black after Cosby's 26.5 seconds, the audio continued. We could hear but not see Cosby reminding me to have a voice over record "Vote for Jesse Jackson for President." We re-directed the spot and had Cosby deliver the tag line.

The Cosby spot was aired immediately. I had bought time in Iowa and New Hampshire in and adjacent to the Cosby Show. The ad was a bomb.

Why? Because Bill Cosby supporting Jesse Jackson was not news. Of course he would be supporting Jackson. After all they are both black.

I learned I needed to find a not-so-obvious endorser.

Gimmicks and Authenticity

Tom Ingram

My first campaign grew out of my experience as a reporter for *The Tennessean* newspaper in 1966 covering Senator Howard Baker's first successful U.S. Senate campaign. It was the first time the Democratic newspaper had ever assigned a reporter to cover a statewide Republican race in Tennessee.

I'm covering the race and toward the end of it a young guy comes home from New York University who has just graduated and becomes the Baker campaign coordinator. His name was Lamar Alexander. We hit it off and became good friends.

In 1974, I left the paper and Lamar asked me to be his press secretary. He was running for Governor. I agreed and that was my first campaign.

It was a textbook campaign, but it didn't have any heart and soul. Lamar looked like an east-coast college chump wearing a blue suit and brown shoes. We got beat by a Congressman from west Tennessee, Ray Blanton.

In 1978, he decides to run again and hires Doug Bailey to be the consultant. Lamar's wife, Honey, and I said we're not going to do another campaign like 1974. We had averaged four hours a day *in an airplane* within the borders of Tennessee taking off and landing, taking off and landing. We told him we were not going to do that again.

One evening we were sitting in his living room talking about what we are going to do differently and somebody asks Lamar, "what do you enjoy doing most when you're out doing what you *want* to do, what do you *enjoy* the most?"

He said "putting on my khakis and boots and walking the Smokies." And Honey said "well, then, why don't you just walk across the state."

After that, the walk idea grew. We decided he should walk in khakis and boots—but you have to have a shirt that is bright so people notice you and something distinctive so they'll recognize you.

So Lamar goes to a surplus store and they had multiple red and black Levi plaid shirts. He brought some home and our reaction was "Great! Perfect!"

We ended up buying fifteen of those shirts and washing them over and over again and hanging them over the back fence so they looked worn. That's how we started the campaign—not knowing at the time that all those shirts and many more would be given away before the campaign was over. The shirts were made in west Tennessee at the Levi's factory and we bought about every shirt they made that year.

So Lamar put on his khakis, boots, and red plaid shirt and starting walking the state.

I learned a couple things from that experience. It put the candidate in an environment where he was genuinely transformed into someone who began *to really hear and understand* what the average Tennessean felt.

He wasn't just going to political events. He went to cattle auctions, high schools, basketball games, and met people across the fence. He'd notice you outside and just stop and talk with you across the fence.

What also happened was that people would come out and talk to him while he was walking. He really began to meet, listen to, and understand Tennesseans.

Everybody wanted to call it a gimmick but gimmicks only work if they're authentic. And there was nothing phony about Lamar Alexander putting on khakis, boots, and a plaid shirt and walking around the state. That's where he was most comfortable.

Getting a Message Across

Tom King

Paul Kirk used to call me in for a meeting once or twice a month when he was chairman of the Democratic Party in 1988—usually he had four or five other people in the room. We would talk about the presidential campaign, and he would ask, "What should we do in response? What's your advice?"

Paul Kirk was a great guy and a smart guy. And he'd say, "We've got to stick with one message." I agreed and said the same thing.

George H. Bush made a tax proposal that would only give middle-class families a $20 tax cut. Michael Dukakis, who was running against him for president, pulls out a $20 bill at an event and shows it to demonstrate what the tax cut would mean to the average family. The media who were there all got video of it—NBC and CBS played it.

Sam Donaldson, who was the anchor of the *ABC Sunday Night News*, wasn't there and missed the shot. So the next day Donaldson gets out a $20 bill and tries to get Dukakis to do it again because ABC missed the visual.

But Dukakis won't do it—the most disciplined man in the world—he won't say the same thing twice. That was part of his problem; he's a smart guy, but smart guys have the hardest time in politics.

They want to say things once and move on. But as Paul Kirk always said—and it's actually an old Kennedy saying: "When your friends and your family refuse to have dinner with you because they've heard the same speech over and over again, *you're just beginning to get your message across.*"

Panda Bear

Jerry Austin

In 1992, I served as senior political advisor to Paul Tsongas's presidential campaign for the Democratic Party nomination.

Tsongas believed that the contest between him and Bill Clinton was about ideas. He wanted to present his plan for America, for Clinton to do the same, and the voters would then decide. He would not allow us to attack Clinton on the air.

While we were in Florida, a state where we had a very weak organization, Clinton ran a television ad criticizing Tsongas for voting to sell warplanes to Saudi Arabia when he was a member of the Senate. Tsongas was livid. I asked if there was anything in the ad that was untrue. He responded, "The ad did not say that six out of the seven senators who are Jewish also voted for the bill." I told him the ad was truthful and they were not required to add the information on the Jewish senators.

I then asked, "Now, can we beat him up?"

"What do you have in mind?" he queried.

Earlier that day I had dispatched an aide to find a stuffed panda bear. I took the panda out of a bag and said to Tsongas, "When we arrive in Fort Lauderdale, I want you to show this bear to the press and state, 'This is what Bill Clinton does. He pandas [ers] to every group he meets.'"

Upon arrival at Fort Lauderdale with the travelling press and local press assembled, Tsongas began his press briefly exhibiting the panda bear with a Clinton sticker affixed to its chest. He said everything we had scripted. The story was the lead on the national newscasts and featured in every newspaper in the country the next day.

On the way in from the airport, a highway patrolman escorting the Tsongas motorcade was killed. Told of the incident, Tsongas suspended campaigning and attended the officer's funeral. He was very depressed. He never thought campaigning for president would take a life.

I had never seen a candidate so shaken by an event. When we resumed campaigning, I handed him the panda bear and told him to repeat his remarks from the previous news conference. We needed to ride the panda bear for the remainder of the campaign.

He refused. He said he was embarrassed that the panda received such a reaction. He wanted his campaign to be about ideas, not gimmicks. He ordered me to never bring up the panda bear again. I never did.

Tsongas never recovered from the patrolman's death. He was never the same candidate. He ran for president having beaten cancer to make the world a better place for his daughters. He never envisioned that a patrolman, a father, would lose his life protecting him.

Human Radar

Ace Smith

If you close your eyes and just listen to President Bill Clinton, you will never hear him use a pause word—ever. Most people say "uh, well, um"—words that people use when they pause to think. You'll never hear that with Clinton.

I didn't quite understand how finely tuned his speaking skills were until I spent a day with him, going from one end of North Carolina to the other, during the primary campaign for Hillary Clinton in 2008.

We must have had ten stops that day; our schedule began at around seven in the morning and went until around ten at night. We started in Greensboro and went all the way out to the far, far west to Asheville in the Blue Ridge Mountains.

Bill Clinton would put all of his remarks on one page of a yellow legal pad. He'd write all these notes, basically just reminders, as an outline. He'd review it once, then he'd just put it aside. He'd do that before starting his speaking schedule for the day and then never look at it again.

During the course of the day he'd go out and give his first speech, testing out his message. He'd have the whole outline in his head, and he'd try it out, and then do something I've never seen anyone else do.

There are very few people who can actually give a speech. And even fewer who can give a *great* speech. Clinton would not only give a great speech but actually monitor the crowd's response at each stop as he's giving the speech, and, on the fly, change it and improve it for the next speech.

Adjusting and improving the speech after every event meant that when he got to the last speech of the day he would be getting applause lines every minute or so. He had literally "market-tested" his material all day long, at every stop, constantly adjusting.

Aside from being an extraordinary speaker and doing it all from memory, extemporaneously, he actually has this rare ability that I've never seen in another politician—he has human radar.

He's sensing the reaction to everything he's saying and he's incorporating it on the fly. It's almost the equivalent of a very talented musician—you can give them a theme and they can improvise something spectacularly.

And he doesn't need to *pause* to adjust the speech, he's mentally three sentences ahead of what he's saying. Once again, like a musician who plays piano or an instrument, he's on the next page, ahead of the notes he's playing.

It makes sense that he has perfected this skill because his background was rural politics in Arkansas where you go from one BBQ to another. It was a skill you had to have in order to connect to people.

The skill he acquired in Arkansas has been lost in the art of public speaking.

Today there is an overdependence on scripted words, so every speech sounds exactly the same. Most speeches are just recited. You lose that spark of spontaneity, the thing that makes it more exciting, the secret ingredient that makes it appear conversational and connects with the audience at an intimate level.

"If We Can't Eat Them, We Shouldn't Shoot Them"
Jeff Plaut

I was polling for a group of animal rights groups in Ohio in 1998 who had gathered signatures to place an issue on the ballot that would make the shooting of mourning doves a crime. It was called the "Save the Dove" campaign.

I conducted our first conference call with the team of the Save the Dove campaign. The groups and team members all stated their general arguments and commented on messaging.

Most of their arguments went something like, "Animals are people. You shouldn't shoot people so you shouldn't shoot animals. Animals are God's children. It's cruel to shoot animals, we shouldn't do it."

They were all stating moral arguments about why it is wrong to shoot animals. This went on for about a half hour.

In the middle of the conversation I realized that one question kept popping into my head, "Who eats mourning doves?"

So I just suddenly blurted out my question. Everyone kind of laughed and said what are you talking about? You don't *eat* mourning doves. The dove has a million little small bones and when they're shot with lead bullets they explode and the dove is filled with bone fragments. It's not eatable, you would choke on it.

I said, "Why don't we try the argument that if we can't eat them we shouldn't shoot them?"

Everyone kind of laughed again, insisting "no, that's not really our argument."

I actually thought that message would make some sense to the voters so I brought it up again but the response was "no, no, no."

When I wrote the poll questions, I put that argument in there and someone mentioned taking it out, but it stayed in.

We conducted the poll and when the results came back it was a tight race and our best argument, by about fifteen points, was my argument that "if you can't eat them, you shouldn't shoot them."

We finished the poll report and then held a meeting where we all talked about what television ad would be most effective.

They essentially had enough money for one poll and one TV ad. There is a certain deference shown to pollsters to at least get a briefing on what the polls say before everyone then gives their opinion.

As a result, I got to go first. I said, "Well, here's what I think we should do. I think we should do an ad with an old couple in front of a McDonald's holding a dead dove in their hands and saying 'if we can't eat them, we shouldn't shoot them.'"

And once again, everyone said, "No, we don't want to do that." We discussed this for about forty-five minutes and I tried everything possible to get them to go with our ad. But they ended up not doing the ad and lost the election 51 percent to 49 percent.

I felt that I had not fought hard enough for my idea. I was upset that I couldn't get them to understand that the argument "if we can't eat them, we shouldn't shoot them" would reverberate with voters.

It also taught me an important lesson. Sometimes when you view the world in one way, you shut out other views. You're just not open to viewing the issue another way. The groups I was working for were fantastic people who cared about the issue but were unwilling to argue the case that would have been most persuasive. And I was unable to convince them.

So that was my experience with the Save the Dove campaign—or perhaps it should have been called the how to "Not Save the Dove" campaign.

Ash Wednesday

John Rendon

The first campaign I worked on was the George McGovern presidential campaign in 1972. My job was to organize college campuses for McGovern. In the first primary I organized volunteers from campuses and brought them to New Hampshire. I got volunteers by running ads in newspapers saying, "We need your body in New Hampshire and not for skiing." The last three weeks before the primary, I sent over twelve hundred students to the Northeast.

After the primary, I left my car in someone's garage in New Hampshire until after the general election, and moved on to Massachusetts.

The Massachusetts primary was the fourth Tuesday in April. Ed Jesser was press secretary and Jerry Vento was director of field operations.

We went to the airport on a Wednesday before Easter to meet McGovern's plane. All of a sudden Jesser realizes, while we are waiting at the gate, that it's Ash Wednesday. And we are in one of the most Catholic states in the country!

So Jesser, without missing a beat, looks over at an ash tray, calls Vento and myself over, and marks all three of us on the forehead using the ashes from the ash tray.

As press secretary, Jesser wasn't about to allow anyone to be in a potential news shot with McGovern who hadn't been to mass on Ash Wednesday.

If you looked at the images you'd see that everyone had been to "mass"—except for McGovern himself, who was a Protestant.

No Cameras, No Story

Tom King

Kevin White, mayor of Boston, was a smart political guy. I was working for the mayor's office in one of the fourteen "Little City Halls" when West Roxbury High School was getting built. We encountered resistance and some protests. The antibusing people didn't want the high school built because they were going to bus in blacks from other neighborhoods to attend the school.

Some antibusing folks are protesting in front of where the school is being built, on Veterans of Foreign Wars parkway. I go down there and my reaction is, "Oh Jesus, it's not that big of a deal but it's going to get on the nightly news."

I get a call to come to the mayor's house for a meeting and there are four of us there: Peter Meade, head of the "Little City Halls" neighborhood outreach; Larry Quealy, secretary to the mayor; and Mickey McDonald, who was the deputy superintendent of police.

We're sitting there trying to decide what to do, and the first person said, "I think we ought to lock them up."

I'm thinking to myself, "Jesus, I don't think we should lock them up. I think we should leave, if there are no cameras, if there's no story—*they'll* leave."

It's tough demonstrating when there's no interest. Before opening my mouth, the next person says, "Kevin why don't we just pull all the police away from there? If there are no police there, there's no story. The protestors will just go away. They'll dissipate."

And I said to myself, "Why didn't I say that? I knew exactly what should be done. Jesus, maybe I do have a future in this."

You Could Not Say That, But I Could

Jerry Austin

The Friday before the New York primary during the 1988 Jackson presidential campaign, I was called by the producer of *This Week with David Brinkley*. They often had Jackson on and since it was a few days before the New York primary it made sense to schedule another appearance.

To my surprise, the producer asked me to appear with New York Mayor Ed Koch representing candidate Al Gore and New York Congressman Charles Schumer representing candidate Michael Dukakis. I could not believe what I was hearing. Campaign managers rarely appear with elected officials. I told the producer I could not believe that the mayor of New York would appear on television, or for that matter anywhere, with Jesse Jackson's campaign manager. He told me a limo would pick me up on Sunday to transport me to the ABC studios. I told him I knew where the studio was and did not need a limo. He said the limo is to make sure I was there on time.

All during the weekend, I was psyching myself down in preparation for my appearance. Over the years, I developed a reputation for "shooting from the lip." There were times when I embarrassed myself and my candidate. I did not want this to happen on national television.

When I arrived at the ABC studios, I was ushered into the proverbial "green room." The room had a table with a terrific spread of food. I made myself my customary Sunday morning bagel and lox sandwich and started to read Sunday's *New York Times.*

Koch and Schumer arrived and I was introduced to them. Koch was taller than I had envisioned. We exchanged some small talk and the producer pulled me aside and said that Koch refused to go on with me. He would be on with the Congressman. I was not surprised. Why would the mayor of New York appear with a campaign manager?

Koch and Schumer left the green room to enter the studio. Although we were all in New York, the journalists, David Brinkley, Cookie Roberts, George Will, and Sam Donaldson were all in Washington, DC. The interview would be conducted by looking in to the camera without the ability to see the other parties.

Brinkley welcomed Koch and before he could ask a question, the mayor began a long diatribe asking how could anyone trust Jesse Jackson. He asked the question, "Was Jesse Jackson with Martin Luther King, Jr. when he died or wasn't he?" Jackson maintained that he was there on the balcony with Dr. King soon after he was shot. Others contended he was in the hotel but was not with him while he lay dying.

Koch monopolized this segment with Schumer saying very little. It appeared to me (I was watching on the monitor in the green room; there was no monitor in the studio) that Brinkley was trying to end this diatribe by Koch. Finally it was time for a commercial. As Koch and Schumer left, I was seated and waited for Brinkley to come back from commercial.

When he returned, Brinkley introduced me and said Sam Donaldson would ask the first question. Donaldson said, "Mr. Austin, you heard Mayor Koch's statement. Was Jesse Jackson with Dr. King when he died or wasn't he?"

I responded, "I don't know, Sam, I wasn't there."

Donaldson fired back, "You're Reverend Jackson's campaign manager, was he there or not?"

I reiterated, "I wasn't there, were you? Were any members of the panel? I wasn't there and I cannot answer the question."

The next question came from George Will. I had always thought Will was a snake. When Jackson was on earlier in the year, Will asked him some detailed question about G7 which no one on the panel knew the answer to. Jackson tried unsuccessfully to BS his way out of it. I told him after the show that he should have attacked Will. He should have said, "George, you're asking me that question to embarrass me. I don't know the answer and neither does anyone else on this panel. But I have a question for you. Is it true your wife put all of your belongings on the front lawn when she found out you were having an affair with Katherine Graham's daughter?"

Jackson cringed and said he would never have said that. Of course, I would have and that's why I was "psyching myself down."

Will's question was, "Mr. Austin, Geraldine Ferraro, your party's vice presidential candidate in 1988 stated this week that Jesse Jackson was running for president just to get the black vote. How do you respond?"

First my reply. Second, what I almost said. It was in my head but fortunately did not come out of my mouth.

I replied, "Ms. Ferraro is wrong. This campaign has attracted voters from every geographic area of the country, from every color of the rainbow and from many blue collar Americans who say Jackson is fighting for them. And, in 1984, Revered Jackson travelled all over the country encouraging people to vote for the Mondale/Ferraro ticket."

What I almost said was: you have to understand that Ms. Ferraro does not like Jesse Jackson. Revered Jackson is very anti-drugs and Ms. Ferraro would not want him as President because it would negatively affect her son's business, who had been arrested for dealing drugs.

The interview ended and I went back to our hotel, where I was confronted by a group of reporters who had just viewed the Brinkley show. I was asked what I thought of Koch's performance. I responded, "Ed Koch is an idiot even by New York standards."

A few hours later, I was standing in one part of the lobby conversing with Bert Lance, when an aide came over to me and said, "Reverend wants to see you." I always found the title "Reverend" used by staff members with the same reverence as "Pope."

I walked across the lobby and joined Jackson. I stood next to him silently and waited for him to speak. He said in a voice just about a whisper, "Did you call Ed Koch a moron?" I said, "No." He encountered, "I was told you called Koch a moron." I said, "No, I called him an idiot."

Jackson admonished me for my remark. He said it was unnecessary. I said it was very necessary. He should not and could not make such a statement but I could. He told me to stop talking to the press.

It was an order I could not follow.

Signs for the Times
Bob Mulholland

Paddy Ashdown, Leader of the Liberal Democrats in the United Kingdom, also known as "Paddy Pantsdown" after the revelation that he had a five-year affair with his secretary, comes down to East Lane, which is the north Yardley district.

I was there to help Baroness Estelle Morris, who was running for reelection to the House of Lords as a member of the Labour party. Paddy was there to push the Liberal Democrats. I told the guys working with me "let's get some signs up."

I was holding a sign that said "Welcome to Yardley, Paddy." So like every good politician he walked straight towards me because I was holding the biggest sign and the media and cameras were all focused on us.

As soon as he got in front of me I said "VOTE LABOUR." He said to me "you son of a bitch." He went on to give his speech which was characterized by the words "ghrrrrrr...you son of a bitch...."

Back in 1994, Bill Clinton was in London meeting with John Major. I talked to the advance people and as he was coming out of Westminster Abbey I put up the sign "California loves Bill Clinton." He came straight towards me and it was all positive messages.

When Tony Blair came to Yardley, I put five people at the event with the sign "Tony, Welcome to Yardley," and the camera picked up those positive signs and messages.

That's what I taught the British people about political activism.

"Meet the New Boss. Same as the Old Boss."

—The Who, "Won't Get Fooled Again," 1971.

Garry South

In the 1994 race for lieutenant governor of California, I was running then-Controller Gray Davis's campaign. We had hired David Axelrod from Chicago to do our paid media.

Axelrod and I had crossed paths years earlier, when I lived in Chicago managing the Alex Seith for U.S. Senate campaign. He was a political reporter at the time with the *Chicago Tribune*.

Davis was well known for forgetting people's names, sometimes confusing one person with someone else—occasionally in very public and embarrassing situations.

One day Davis and I went in to talk with the *Bakersfield Californian* editorial board. The newspaper headquarters is located in downtown Bakersfield in an old, historic building, with a conference room that looks like it could be in a Tudor mansion, with a painted ceiling and a big fireplace with a heraldic decoration on it.

Gray sits down at the big conference table with the editorial staff, and I take a seat against the wall. Before he gets started, he says, "I would like to introduce you to my campaign manager, Garry South. He used to be in your business, he was a political reporter at the *Chicago Tribune*."

He had, obviously, totally confused my background with that of David Axelrod, his media consultant. I needed to somehow correct the record because I hadn't been a reporter since my college newspaper days! And I never worked for the *Chicago Tribune.*

I did some quick thinking, trying to figure out how to explain away the confusion without making Davis look like a fool.

I didn't want to leave the impression out there that he didn't know who his own campaign manager was.

I stood up, stammered, and finally uttered something like, "Uh, I did live in Chicago at one time, and worked, uh, with the *Tribune* on a, uh, political campaign."

Luckily, no one followed up and asked me about it.

But, as I soon discovered, that was only the beginning of Davis getting people—including me—mixed up.

After he was elected governor in 1998, a campaign I also ran, I was at a transition meeting where he referred to me as *Jerry.*

Davis had been chief of staff to Governor Jerry Brown for six and half years from 1975 to 1981.

I interrupted him and asked, "*Jerry?*"

He looked puzzled for a moment, like he didn't understand why I was questioning him. Then he said, "Oh, of course, I mean Garry."

After he left, all of us in the room had a good laugh about his confusion. One participant quoted a famous line from a song by *The Who.*

"That's a Freudian slip that means he really sees you as his boss, as in 'New boss, same as the old boss!'"

The Gang of Five

Alice Huffman

Willie Brown, the Speaker of the California State Assembly, taught me some very important lessons early in my political career. First of all he's one of the brightest people you'll ever know. He is not just bright intellectually but he's smart politically, which is a combination that you don't see too often. In politics you encounter either brilliant people or smart people. He's a bright and smart guy.

While everybody else is politicking to get a new program passed, he's already thinking about how to make that program work. If you look at the relationship he had with his members when he was Speaker, he had love on both sides of the aisle and that was how he got things done. That's why California government really worked and worked in a bipartisan way.

When Willie Brown was at the height of his popularity and power, he took care of several Republicans. He never, ever left them completely out of the loop even though he knew he could. When Willie Brown's mother passed, I went to the funeral and noticed that some of the right-wing Republicans were at the funeral.

Now you could say that was just protocol, but when you saw Willie with them after hours, you realized these guys were *buddies*. They were hand-slapping, and "hey, how you doin,'" really friendly towards each other. But during business hours at the State Assembly you'd never know it.

When I was at the California Teachers Association (CTA) Willie Brown had a fight with Dianne Feinstein. Willie Brown would call me up whenever he had a disagreement with someone because he knew how powerful the teachers were.

So whenever he wanted an ally on his side he'd call me. On this occasion, he was really mad at Dianne Feinstein because he felt she had disrespected him on some issue.

Just a couple of months later I read in the papers that Willie Brown was seen having lunch with Dianne Feinstein.

I had to ask myself, "Why am I getting these teachers all mad at Feinstein because of the way she treated Willie and he's out having an amicable lunch with her?" I just let it slide but I should have realized at the time that it was an important lesson on how Willie operates.

On another occasion, Willie called me up about the *gang of five*. The *gang of five* consisted of five Democratic members of the State Assembly who were trying to oust Willie. I made sure the CTA didn't give those members any campaign money.

Then I discover, little by little, Willie Brown was putting those guys back in positions of power. So I went to him and I said, "Willie, you've really thrown me to the curb here. So let me ask you, these people treat you like dirt, they're trying to oust you and you turn around and make a way for them to come back into your administration?"

He said, "Listen Huffman, I want you to know something. If you get too many people on the outside you set yourself up for a coup. You don't bring them into your inner circle *but you've got to bring them back in.* You can't let them stay out there because the more they stay out there, the more trouble they make for you.

"When you have power and authority, you're going to offend some people. But don't let them linger out there. Don't let them get enough people out there so they can topple you."

That was an important lesson, and I use it all the time in my work now. He also reminded me that the members of the *gang of five* have not fared well. If you go back and look at what's happened to each one—they've all in one way or the other met their coming down. You could go through each one of them and see that they didn't fare well in the end.

The Rise of Dick Morris

Jerry Austin

In 1975, during Dick Celeste's term as lieutenant governor of Ohio, I served as chief of staff. The title had more importance than the job. The lieutenant governor at that time was elected separately from the governor, and had as his only responsibility to preside over the Senate and vote only in case of a tie. The other function of being commander-in-chief of the Ohio Navy had become outdated.

Our small staff of five, with a biennial budget of under $150,000, spent most of our time learning about state government and promoting the lieutenant governor.

One day, I noticed two unfamiliar names on the schedule: Dick Morris and Dick Dresner. I asked the scheduler who they were and what they wanted. I was told they were New York pollsters who were looking for business in Ohio.

I invited myself to the meeting. After a recitation of their bios, I asked why they were in Columbus. Morris responded that they had researched the rising stars of the Democratic Party. They concluded that the lieutenant governor of Ohio, a Rhodes scholar and Yale graduate and/or the attorney general of Arkansas, a Rhodes scholar and Yale (Law School) graduate, would become president of the United States before the end of the century. They volunteered that both candidates (Dick Celeste and Bill Clinton) were very bright, good looking, great campaigners, extremely articulate and charismatic.

After the meeting, I made sure Morris and Dresner never saw Celeste again—although Morris did date the scheduler for awhile.

Morris's name resurfaced years later after he had become a stealth advisor to Clinton during the 1992 campaign. Eventually, he became well known as a pollster and advisor to Republicans as well.

Soon after Ron Brown was named as secretary of commerce designee by Clinton, Morris called me. He had received my phone number from Hank Sheinkopf, my partner at the time, and an old friend of Dick's. He wanted me to arrange for him to meet Ron Brown. I asked why and he responded that Brown would appear before Senator Trent Lott's committee for confirmation. Lott was a client of his and Morris wanted to be helpful.

I told Morris I would call Ron, tell him of his interest in meeting, and give Brown his telephone number. Brown would call if he was interested.

I had met Ron Brown years before at a conference I attended in Barbados. Ron had a reputation of being very bright, charming, and good looking. I did not see him again until after I was appointed Jackson's campaign manager. He had asked that we meet the next time I was in Washington, DC.

When we met, he offered his services as a volunteer advisor. We talked often and he became one of Jackson's closest advisors. Eventually, he would become Jackson's convention manager.

I told Ron of my conversation with Morris. He asked what Morris really wanted. I responded that he probably wanted to ingratiate himself to Ron and then visit him as Secretary with one of his clients.

Prior to appearing before Lott's committee, the rumor was that Brown would be the most likely cabinet designee to fail to win Senate confirmation. There were a number of questions regarding Brown's business dealings. However, Brown's appearance before the committee was nothing but smooth sailing.

Did Ron and Dick talk? Probably. Did Dick deliver Lott? Probably.

How I Became Political Director

Paul Curcio

I actually started out in product advertising. I got my MBA from UCLA. From there I went to New York and worked for an advertising agency. I worked on the name brands but I found that I wasn't really interested in all that.

In 1984, I had an opportunity to go to Washington, DC, because a guy who had come to work at the advertising agency had just left his position as Chief of Staff to Millicent Fenwick, Congresswoman from New Jersey. He knew people in DC and said, "I'll set you up with information and interviews and we'll see what comes of it."

One of the people he set me up with was a guy named Mitch Daniels, who went on to become the governor of Indiana. At the time he was executive director of the National Republican Senatorial Committee (NRSC). It turned out that he needed somebody who knew something about politics and something about advertising.

It was literally one of those situations in life where you're in the right place at the right time and you have to make a choice.

I had never really worked on a campaign. But I got a low-level job at the NRSC with an eleven-month commitment. Ultimately that short-term job turned into eleven years with the committee.

In 1990 Senator Phil Gramm, Republican from Texas, was elected chairman of the NRSC.

He's a street fighter, a brawler, which we needed at the time because even though we had a popular Republican president and more money than our Democratic counterpart, we kept losing Senate races all through the 1980s.

Gramm comes in and conducts his first meeting at the NRSC building with all the political staff—everybody was supposed to be in the room from midlevel on up.

I was sort of midlevel at best—the more important staff sat around the table with Gramm at the head of the table. Since I was midlevel I sat around the perimeter.

Gramm comes in and he peers out over his glasses, and he has this reputation that he'll mow you over and he doesn't want to hear contrary things. Neither of which is true, it's actually the opposite. He does want to hear contrary things—you just have to be able to back it up.

He says, "Everything is going to be different here—I'm going to do things differently—it's going to be much more hands-on." And everyone is getting scared, assuming we're all going to lose our jobs.

Then he states the obvious. "Now I want to know why all through the 1980s we had a popular president, we had more money, we had good candidates, why are we steadily losing all these senate seats?" Total silence. And he said, "Well, why is this?"

He looks around at the staff seated around the table. It felt like the silence went on forever. It was obvious that everyone was frightened and nobody wanted to say a word.

I figured, what the hell, we're all going to get fired anyway. So I said, "I've got some thoughts." And he peers over his glasses and says, "Well, who are you?"

I said, "I'm Paul Curcio." He tells me to proceed. So I said, "I think there are really four main reasons." I don't remember anymore what the reasons were but I went through them.

After I finished speaking he says, "Anybody else? Anyone else have anything to say?" And nobody else had anything to add, so he was agitated. He ran through some other business and then he leaves and goes back to his Senate office.

About a week later he says to the temporary executive director, who was a long-time aide of his, "I want to come over to the NRSC. Get that same group together."

They come over, him and his aide, who ultimately became the executive director. He enters the room, and does the same thing, he starts asking questions and once again nobody's saying a word. I thought, "Well, this time we really *are* going to get fired."

Once again I raised my hand and said, "I think there are a couple of things." This time he challenged me—"I don't think that's true"—and told me why. I responded, "Senator, I think it *is* true," and I explained my reasons—you could tell he was agitated. The meeting ends without anyone else speaking up. Now you could tell he's really steamed. He gets up and leaves.

Gramm goes back to his Senate office and he calls over his aide and he has the roster of everybody in the political division.

Gramm says to Jeb, "You got a pen? The following people are going to be fired." He named the executive director, political director, all of the old staff, the assistant field people—everybody.

He said, "You got this fellow Curr-rach-io." He never could get my name right. "Curr-rach-io—put him in charge."

I had never even worked on a campaign before, but that's how I became political director. On the basis of two meetings and two exchanges with a chairman who couldn't even pronounce my last name.

I was his political director for two election cycles, 1992 and 1994. During that time we captured a Republican majority in the Senate with a gain of eight seats and reversed a decade-long decline.

Getting Some Guidance

Alice Huffman

The thing about working for California Governor Jerry Brown is that you really don't see much of him. If you work in his administration, you get your opinion of Jerry mostly by what you read in the papers and perhaps one or two special meetings.

I remember one meeting with him when he was governor back in the late 1970s. It was fairly early into his first term and he had a good record of the number of minorities and women he put into judicial positions. I think the African Americans had a little bit of a lead on the Latinos, but he was pretty good about trying to make sure that the diversity of the state was reflected in his administration.

He had hired about twelve blacks for top positions: one was over at the Department of Social Services, one was at Health and Welfare, one was a special assistant in his office, a Latino was also over at Health and Welfare, I was the deputy director of Parks and Recreation, and a black guy was director of Parks and Recreation. So he had done a pretty good job with his appointments.

Now, as I said, if you work for Jerry you really don't see a lot of him. And the guy at the Department of Social Services and others kept telling me, "we need a meeting with the governor, we need a meeting with the governor." I assured them we'd get a meeting with the governor and set it up.

The governor had all of us come into his conference room for the meeting. When he walked in he didn't have any preliminary comments or introduction to the meeting, he just said, "What's this about?"

As spokesperson for the group I said, "Mr. Governor, we've been working for you for some time now, for maybe four or five months, and we really need some guidance. We really want to know what you are about and what you want us to do."

He said, "I'll tell you what I'm about. I'm about to tell you that I hired the wrong people. If you don't know what to do after living in America all your lives, don't ask me," and walked out.

That was his response. I was embarrassed for all of us. I mean the message was so pointed. How can he tell us that he appointed all of us to these agencies to do a job, but it's absurd for us to seek guidance from him?

I never forgot that meeting and his words. That was a real lesson. The few times I saw him under his administration I admired him; I adored him. I thought he was the most dynamic guy I'd ever seen. People called him "Governor Moonbeam" and all of that crazy stuff, but he was real. He was for the people just as he is now. He did things that nobody else would dare try.

Changing the Primary Date

John Rendon

The Massachusetts presidential primary had historically been held on the fourth Tuesday in April. In 1976, it was moved up to the first Tuesday in March to be part of "Super Tuesday."

A decision was made within the 1980 Carter presidential reelection campaign that strategically it would be better to move the primary back to April. Ed King, a center-right, conservative Democrat, was governor of Massachusetts at the time and did not like Ted Kennedy, Carter's rival. So King was in favor of moving the primary back to April because it would help Carter and hurt Kennedy.

So I get my instructions from the campaign to go up to Massachusetts, since I'm from there, and move the Massachusetts primary from the first Tuesday in March back to the fourth Tuesday in April.

I make a few phone calls and arrange to meet with the legislative leadership on Saturday. I took the Eastern Airlines shuttle up making sure I wasn't being followed and take the "T" (the subway) to Bowdoin Street, walking past my old parking space from when I was a special assistant to former Democratic governor, Mike Dukakis.

I walk through the door to the Statehouse, walking past the pay phone that's off to the left. On the marble you can hear my footsteps three centuries away. Since it was a Saturday, nobody was there. I go up the marble steps which were pitted from all the people who had walked up them before me.

I walk onto the floor of the House of Representatives, and the Speaker Tommy McGee from Lynn, MA, is sitting there with other legislators. I try to get his attention, "Mr. Speaker!" He doesn't notice me so I try again, "Mr. Speaker!"

He finally looks up and says, "Jackie, how are ya?" To which I responded "Mr. Speaker, good to see ya."

The Speaker said "What can we do for ya?"

"Mr. Speaker, you know historically, the Commonwealth of Massachusetts, one of the four Commonwealths in the United States, holds its presidential primary on the fourth Tuesday in April, and last time, in 1976, it came up early. A couple of us were just wondering what you thought about moving it back to its rightful place on the fourth Tuesday in April?"

McGee looks around and says, "Well, I don't see a problem with that. What do you guys think?"

The legislators say, "We'll do whatever you want, Mr. Speaker."

McGee says, "All right, you got it. What day do you want the change to come up?"

I said, "Mr. Speaker, I want it on Wednesday."

He said, "Okay, you got it on Wednesday."

I then proceeded to tell him, "Now look—I'm going to walk across the hall and talk to your colleagues in the Senate, but *Mr. Speaker, I came to you first.*"

He nods and says, "We know that Jackie."

I go across the hall to see the Senate president, Kevin Harrington. I state my case and say to Kevin Harrington, "Mr. President, you're the *first* guy I'm talking to about moving the Massachusetts primary."

Harrington said, "We're also wondering about changing the date of the Massachusetts primary back to its rightful place historically. So what day would you like us to address it?"

I said, "I think it's pretty good if you bring it up on Tuesday."

He said, "Okay, we'll give you all three readings on Tuesday."

I said, "Good. I'm going to talk to the House and see if they'll bring it up on Wednesday."

I walk back over to the House and I said, "Mr. Speaker, I've just come from your colleagues across the way, in the other chamber, and they've agreed to go on Tuesday if that's okay with you."

He said, "Great, we'll do all three readings on Wednesday and have the bill to the governor on Thursday."

I said, "Good, the governor will sign on Friday."

Done. I shake hands with everybody, you know—"See y'all later." I walk out thinking to myself, "Well, that went pretty good." I walk by and I see the pay phone again, but decide that I'm not going to call from that one.

I walk down Bowdoin Street and I remember that the address John Kennedy used when he was president was on Bowdoin Street. I'm thinking about all these symbols. I'm walking past and I go all the way down to the end of Bowdoin Street to use the pay phone there.

I get the White House operator on the phone and I ask for Camp David. I get the Camp David operator and ask for Hamilton Jordan. I said "Mr. Jordan? Mr. Rendon calling. I'm calling you from the bottom of Bowdoin Street in Boston. Right down the street from the Statehouse.

"I've just left their leadership and they have agreed to move the Massachusetts primary back to its rightful place historically, on the fourth Tuesday in April."

Jordan says, "Rendon, I've talked to the President, and we don't think this is such a good idea." I said, "Excuse me?" He said, "I don't think this is a good idea. It'll look like we're tampering with the system."

I said, "Hamilton—we *are* tampering with the system!" He said, "Go back and get them to change their plans and just leave it where it is in March."

So I go right back up the hill and they're still there—all I have to do is get one of them to stop the change. I go in and I say, "Mr. Speaker," and he said, "Jackie?

What're you doing back?" And I say, "Look, I just talked to the president and he's *really* appreciative of your offer to move the primary, but he doesn't think it is necessary." Now McGee knows he's got me.

He again replies, saying, "Ahh, that's all right. We don't mind moving it."

I said, "No, Mr. Speaker, it's *really* important that it not be moved." He repeats that, "We don't mind doing it. It's really okay." I'm thinking, "What is it going to take to get them to not move it?"

The primary doesn't move back to April. It stayed in March and it's still in March today.

After Carter loses reelection, I run into McGee at a fundraising event and I said to him, "Mr. Speaker, you've got to tell me the truth. Why were you so willing to move the primary? I know we're friends and all that, but I also know this wasn't about me."

He said, "Jackie, it's really easy to understand. Every one of my members knows Jimmy Carter and many of them have never even met Ted Kennedy."

Another lesson in "all politics is local." And a very important lesson: *don't take anything for granted.*

Convention Madness

Rick Rendon

In 1980, I was working as a field organizer for the Carter/Mondale reelection campaign. After the primaries were over we were all preparing for the National Democratic Convention in New York City.

I was brought back to Washington, DC, and became one of the delegate trackers. I was given eight states where I was supposed to track delegates. Basically my job was to make sure we didn't lose any delegates to Ted Kennedy and make sure they would support President Carter's platform on issues.

That is all I did that summer. I called up delegates. I befriended them. I sent them personal notes. I flew out to their state to meet with them. I did briefings with the delegations. I got to know their families. I took care of their every need.

During the convention I was on the floor running around from state to state with my little delegate book and I'm having a problem with the delegation in Wyoming.

We get word that the Kennedy folks are going to try to do a last-minute effort to open up the convention in the hope that some delegates would switch their support from Carter to Kennedy. The entire convention comes down to this one, *really critical* vote.

The trackers are all crowded into the delegate trailer where we had these point-to-point phones; direct lines so you could pick up a phone, dial a state delegation, and be connected to the head of the delegation—usually the governor.

Suddenly Hamilton Jordan comes into the trailer and says, "Ok everybody, the vote's coming down shortly, we got any problems out there?"

And I said, "Yes, Hamilton, I think we have a problem with Wyoming." Wyoming was one of my states. "It seems like we're losing some delegates in Wyoming."

Hamilton immediately says, "Son, get over to the command trailer." If Hamilton Jordan tells you to run off a bridge, you're going to run off the bridge.

I go running over to the command trailer. The most critical vote of the convention is coming down and I'm losing delegates! I burst into the command trailer, not even thinking about who was going to be there. I just burst right through the door and sitting around the table is the "*high command*"—Jody Powell, Walter Mondale, and Bob Strauss.

Strauss looks up at me and says, "Son, what are you doing?"

I'm so out of breath I can barely get the words out. "Sir, Mr. Strauss sir, Hamilton Jordan sent me over here to tell you that we're having a problem with the delegates in Wyoming."

Keep in mind that I'm only twenty-four years old and my only job that summer, the *entire summer*, was to keep my delegates in line. The last three months, I've flown across the country to meet with these delegates. I've had dinner with these delegates, I've sent them personal notes, birthday cards, you name it—I know *everything* about them.

Strauss says, "Son, get me the governor on the phone."

I pick up the direct-line phone and call the Wyoming delegation. "Governor Herschler, Rick Rendon here, Bob Strauss would like to talk to you."

Strauss gets on the phone and I can hear him saying, "What's going on? We got a problem in Wyoming? Uh huh, uh huh, uh huh. Ok. Put Tom on the phone."

"Tommy, this is Bob Strauss. Now, me and the president are coming out to Wyoming and we're goin' fishin' with the governor. Okay? But I'll be damned if you're coming along unless you're with us on this vote. Ok. Good. Uh huh. Put Mikey on the phone."

"Mikey, I just talked to Tommy. Now, the governor, the president and I, we're all going fishin' and we want you to come along, but guess what, you ain't comin' with us unless you vote right. Good. Ok. Uh huh. Put Joe on the phone."

"Joe, this is the last offer I'm going to make to you, we're all goin' fishin' with the president, you can come along. But if you walk off the reservation, you won't be part of it. Ok? Uh huh. Good."

He hands me the phone and says, "Son, hang up the phone and get the hell out of here."

I spent three months lobbying these folks, I've practically lived with them, and all Strauss had to do was *go fishing*.

Convention Chaos

Jerry Austin

During the summer of 1968, I was enjoying time off from teaching. I had been an early supporter of Senator Eugene McCarthy's bid for the Democratic presidential nomination. I also detested Senator Robert Kennedy's late entrance into the race after McCarthy had embarrassed President Lyndon Johnson in the New Hampshire primary.

I received a phone call asking if I would be a volunteer driver for Senator George McGovern who had become a candidate for president soon after Bobby Kennedy had been assassinated. His quest for the presidency was more symbolic than real. He was appearing in Cleveland on his way to the Chicago convention. I quickly agreed to volunteer myself and my 1966 Plymouth Valiant to be part of the McGovern motorcade.

I quickly learned that being a motorcade volunteer took a good deal of patience. Your job was to drive, in my case, a group of McGovern staff people to and from the events of the day. You drove and waited outside the event and proceeded to the next event. After the last event was over, on the return trip to the airport, one of the staffers asked me to come to the convention in Chicago. He said there was a need for volunteers and I would find the convention very interesting and exciting.

I decided to volunteer. Flights between Chicago and Cleveland were fairly cheap. Before leaving for the convention, I checked in with Dick Celeste, who was planning to attend the convention and begin a Draft Ted Kennedy movement. His rationale was that Humphrey could win the nomination and not the election, and McCarthy could win the election and not the nomination. He told me if I wanted to participate to meet him in his room at the Sherman House Hotel on Sunday night.

I arrived at the convention and took the bus from the airport to the McGovern hotel on Michigan Avenue. I was astounded by the large number of volunteers who were hanging around. After a few hours, I realized that this was not the place for me.

On Sunday night I joined Celeste and about a dozen people at the Sherman House. Celeste led the meeting and announced that he had secured the suite of former Governor of Ohio, Mike DiSalle, to serve as Draft Kennedy Headquarters. He asked me if I would man the suite, which included staying overnight in the bedroom portion of the suite. I said yes. Before the meeting broke up, assignments were given to those in attendance to contact various delegations and inform them of the draft movement.

A state senator from Alabama named Tom Radney told those assembled that he had called the local media back home and told them of his plan to participate in a Draft Teddy Kennedy movement at the convention. Just before he left to catch his plane the phone rang. He answered and the person on the line said, "Roses are red; violets are blue; two Kennedys are dead and so are you."

I volunteered with a young man from Iowa to put up signs on every floor of every convention hotel on Michigan Avenue announcing the locations of the Draft Kennedy Headquarters location. This was a much larger job than I had envisioned. The last hotel was done after three a.m. I returned to the DiSalle suite to retire.

At seven-thirty a.m. there was a knock at the door. Still in a not-enough-sleep fog, I answered the door and was greeted by a crowd of about ten people in the hallway. They represented various delegations and wanted to volunteer. I invited them in and asked if they would identify delegates in their state delegations who might be persuaded to vote for Ted Kennedy. I also grabbed a trash can and put a makeshift sign inside that said "donations." The flow of people lasted all day and into the night.

By the end of the day, I had enough money to dispatch a volunteer to Indiana to purchase ten thousand buttons left over from the Indiana primary. The buttons had white letters on a light blue background and they said "Kennedy." They were the size of a nickel. When the volunteer returned I dispatched other volunteers to the lobbies of the convention hotels to sell the "Kennedy" buttons for $1 apiece.

They were sold in two hours. I used the new money to have large "Edward Kennedy for President" buttons designed. These were produced within twenty-four hours and the volunteers were dispatched again to convention hotels, although the asking price was now $5.

Meanwhile, Celeste had been meeting with Kennedy friends and advising them of the momentum we were witnessing. At the same time, the "police riot" started in the streets outside the convention hall. I tried to leave the Sherman House by elevator but the protesters had thrown stink bombs down the shaft. I proceeded to the stairs. As I was walking down the stairs a group of Chicago policeman stopped me and asked for my ID. I showed him my Ohio's driver's license and he said that since I was wearing a tie and jacket even though I had a beard, he would let me go.

I exited to the street and on to Michigan Avenue. The sight was unforgettable. Chicago police were everywhere. They were chasing people, firing tear gas into crowds, and beating protesters. I returned to the Draft Headquarters where Celeste was on the phone. He informed me that the Kennedy family wanted the Draft stopped. We quickly stopped the Draft campaign and began a campaign to raise money to bail the protesters out of jail. We called a quick meeting of volunteers. They were sent to the convention hotels to raise money from the delegates as they returned from the convention hall.

I went to the California delegation's hotel. Because of the size of the delegation, we had many volunteers armed with homemade signs asking for donations to free the protesters. Many also had garbage cans to deposit the donations.

I spotted the delegation leader, Speaker of the California Assembly Jesse Unruh. I walked towards him. Without stopping or speaking, he took a bill from his wallet and placed it in the garbage can I was holding. As he passed by and I uttered "thank you," I looked inside the can and saw a $100 bill.

The fundraising was very successful. We turned over almost $10,000 to the legal team representing the protesters.

The next day, Celeste and I decided to head back to Cleveland. We did not want to be in Chicago any longer. The only seats available on the next flight to Cleveland were in first class. I had some money left over. Milton Shapp, a future Governor of Pennsylvania had given Celeste $500 for the Draft and Mike DiSalle had done the same. We bought the first-class tickets and boarded the plane for the one-hour trip to Cleveland. In those days, first-class passengers received a steak dinner and as much of the beverage of your choice as you wished to consume.

Celeste and I started downing Jack Daniels as well as a small bottle of wine. When we arrived in Cleveland, we were half drunk. We took a taxi to Celeste's home where we announced to our retrospective wives that we were going to work for Nixon. We believed the Democratic Party had to be destroyed and then built anew.

We sobered up in the morning and both worked for the Humphrey-Muskie ticket.

III. Wry and Wise

Presidential Impersonation

Jerry Austin

In 1980, the Carter/Mondale campaign assigned me to run downstate Illinois during the March Democratic primary. This was an important primary not only because it was in a big state but also because it was early in the primary season. In addition, Ted Kennedy initially was favored to win the state because of his family's long-time ties to the Daleys of Chicago.

Downstate was every part of the state except the Chicago area. After the Iowa caucuses, the best Carter organizers were assigned to Illinois. Among the staff I inherited was Rick Rendon, a twenty-one-year-old from Boston, who was the younger brother of John Rendon, the campaign scheduler.

I assigned Rick to southern Illinois and he moved to Carbondale. About once a week during the two and half months I spent running the downtown operation out of Springfield, I would receive a phone call from Rick impersonating Ted Kennedy.

We shut out Kennedy in downstate and I moved on to Ohio, bringing Rick and most of my Illinois staffers with me. I assigned Rick to Cincinnati. He continued to call and impersonate Senator Kennedy. We beat Kennedy in Ohio while Carter lost to him in New Jersey and California on the same first Tuesday in June. The Ohio win assured President Carter the Democratic Party nomination.

In the fall, I was assigned to Ohio. Many of my star staffers were given small states or major roles in larger states. Rick Rendon was assigned to my old job of coordinating downstate Illinois. Instead of calling me once a week to imitate Kennedy, he would call once a month. The call was different.

I would pick up the phone and a very officious woman's voice would ask, "Is this Mr. Austin?" I would reply "yes" and would be told, "Please hold for the President of the United States." I would wait for about thirty seconds and Rick would come on imitating President Carter. The first time he called I really thought it was the president.

After the campaign was over, I remained in Columbus, my home, and Rick returned to Boston. It was a depressing time. Carter had lost to Reagan and all of the campaign staffers were unemployed without many leads on future employment.

On the Friday after Thanksgiving, I was in my apartment when the phone rang late in the afternoon. I answered and that officious voice asked, "Is this Mr. Austin?" I responded, "Yes," with a bit of a chuckle in my voice. As I waited to hear the next voice on the phone, I recalled how much enjoyment Rick had given me all year with him impersonations.

After what seemed like a long time, the voice said, "Jerry, Jimmy. I just wanted to call and thank you for all the work you did for me in Ohio. I really appreciate your efforts."

Playing along, I responded, "Mr. President, how is Roslyn taking the loss?"

He said, "She's taking it very hard—very hard."

I said sarcastically, "You know what they say? How you gonna keep 'em down on the farm after they've seem Paree."

There was a long pause. And the voice said, "Jerry, this is Jimmy Carter." I pretended I did not make my "paree" remark, thanked the president for his call and hung up.

Eight years later, after running Jesse Jackson's presidential campaign, I was invited to Cincinnati to a fundraising dinner for the Carter Center. The ticket price was high and the attendance was low.

The host introduced all of the attendees as President Carter acknowledged each person with a handshake. He shook my hand and went on to the next two contributors, then suddenly stopped and reversed himself. He came back to me and said, "Paree."

A Good Hand Man

Bob Keefe

Following our defeat in the 1972 presidential election, Bob Strauss became chairman of the National Democratic Party and I became executive director.

Strauss had made a commitment to one of his friends, Senator Henry "Scoop" Jackson from Washington, to run Jackson's campaign for president in 1976.

Late fall of 1975, Strauss calls me in and says, "Bob I made this commitment to Jackson that I would run his campaign and I don't think I can do that. Do you think I should go run Jackson's campaign?"

I said, "I don't think that would be wise."

Without missing a beat, Strauss says, "Then you're going to do it."

He takes me over to Scoop Jackson's office and tells him he can't run his campaign so I was going to do it for him.

So I get the pleasant assignment to go involve myself in the Jackson campaign and the first thing I had to do was go to Florida for a weekend.

I went to Florida on a Friday because on Sunday my wife had planned to have a bunch of people over for brunch. I remember telling her I wouldn't have to travel much. "Don't worry about it. No change. Everything is fine."

I go to Florida to meet the campaign team in the state and on Sunday morning I catch the first plane home, getting to the house about an hour before everyone arrives for brunch.

Attempting to be a good thoughtful husband, I said I would put the orange juice and champagne together for the mimosas, and WAM! I slice my finger off. I literally cut a tendon in my finger on the lid of an orange juice can and have to be rushed to the hospital.

That weekend is really the first memory I have of the Jackson campaign.

One of the things about Scoop was that he was very involved with the medical community. He should have been a doctor. If you had a pimple, a hemorrhoid, or cancer he had the perfect guy to handle it.

It drove him nuts figuring out how to best get my finger repaired. He had me go to doctors in three or four places—New York, Los Angeles, Boston. It's very tough surgery. Hand surgery is the most difficult surgery there is.

This went on for months and finally one morning he called and said, "I found the guy!" It was this guy from Nevada who had a son who was in a car accident that severed his hand and he told Scoop he knew exactly where I should go.

So what do they suggest? Walter Reid Hospital in Washington, DC. It turns out that Walter Reid does have a very good *hand* man.

My hand has worked beautifully ever since.

The Sweepstakes

David Heller

I was the media consultant to Democratic Congressman John Olver from Massachusetts. In 1998, during Olver's reelection campaign, I wrote a television ad featuring the Congressman posed at various geographic sites in the district. The last site to be filmed was in the town of Conway.

The consultant, congressman, campaign manager, and camera crew all arrived in Conway. We wanted to shoot the congressman posed with the proprietors of an antique store. We especially wanted a store that had a sign entitled "CONWAY ANTIQUES." They looked up antique stores in the Yellow Pages and found one store with the name they sought.

The Congressman wanted to call the owner and ask if they could come by and shoot the ad with him and the owners in front of the sign. I cautioned that it would be better to drive to the store and make sure the sign and the building were worth shooting.

We proceeded to the store in a caravan of four cars and we were thrilled that the sign was in front of a home which also served as the place of business for CONWAY ANTIQUES.

I asked the camera crew to begin setting up in front of the sign. The campaign manager and I approached the front door. We rang the doorbell and an older woman peeked from behind the door. She noticed the camera crew setting up on the lawn. She opened the door and called out to her husband, "We won the Publishers Clearing House Sweepstakes."

A Pollster Not an Upholsterer

Jeff Plaut

The 2010 election cycle was very bad for Democrats around the country. Following the election there were a lot of conferences and symposiums on what happened in it and where do we go from here.

At one of the conferences where I was a panelist, I was standing off to the side waiting for my session to begin, when a middle-aged woman comes running up to me and very enthusiastically says, "I need to talk to you about my living room." I was perplexed by the question and asked why she was asking about her living room.

She looked at me kind of emphatically and said, "They told me you were an upholsterer and I want to talk to you about my living room!"

I laughed and told her, "This is a political conference not a redecorating conference. I am a pollster not an upholsterer. We do representative samples in swing districts. We don't do sofas and living rooms."

Apparently she didn't need a pollster.

Gary's Gorillas

John Toohey

In 1984, Tom Hogue was running Pennsylvania for Gary Hart's presidential campaign. His right-hand man was Martin O'Malley, who went on to become governor of the state of Maryland.

Hogue has got this idea that he's going to bring someone into the campaign that is a little off-the-wall to handle people coming into the state and do special projects discreetly. Someone suggested me. Hogue didn't know who I was, but he took their word for it.

We have all these people coming in and Hogue gives me some money and gets me a plane so I can fly around the state, basically whatever I wanted I got. My work in the state was supposed to be under the radar because it involved some activities you didn't want made public.

We called these volunteers "Gary's Gorillas" and for two weekends in a row it was fantastic. One weekend there's this really big story in the paper. The story wasn't really about me but it was about "Gary's Gorillas," which is bad enough—but I'm in the story too. I mean, I'm *really* in the story and that's bad.

I see the Sunday paper that morning and I debate not even going into the office. First, I'm just humiliated and angry with myself for being such a rookie. How did this happen? There are even quotes from me.

But I figure Hogue has been really good to me, he's given me all this rope to hang myself, and he's entitled to pull the trap door. I figure I have to man up, go in, and get fired.

Hogue's office was set up so you didn't see it when you walked into the campaign headquarters. But he could see everyone else.

I came walking in—I thought about bringing my bags with me—but I didn't want to be a defeatist. I wander around the office to see if anyone else mentions the article.

I hear Hogue call out, "Hey, Toohey, come on in here son!"

I figure I'm fired for sure. I slowly walk myself to Hogue's office.

Hogue says, "Hey, you see this morning's paper?" I just nod my head.

"What did you think about that? Not bad, but not good. Could have been a whole lot better, but could have been a whole lot worse!"

I nod again.

"You learn something from all this, son? You got to be careful son. You need any money? That's a good boy—just make sure you get the receipts."

Apologizing to Protestants

Nancy Korman

One time Senator Ted Kennedy and I were at a fundraiser, a buffet down on Cape Cod. Ted asked me, "Nancy, what is that on that table?" I said, "That's lobster salad." He said, "But there are Jewish people here, what if they don't eat lobster?" So I told him, "On the other table there's chicken salad and vegetarian platters." And he responded, "Oh, good job."

Ted was also willing to take criticism and process it. He never blew you off just because you were in opposition to his position.

He once hosted the Democratic National Campaign Committee. There was a Senator at each table and a mixed group of people at the event. Before beginning, the invocation was given in the name of the Father, the Son, and the Holy Ghost.

I walked up to Ted during the dinner and I said, "Ted, you can do a Christian prayer at Thanksgiving or any time you eat at Ethel Kennedy's house, but you can't do one at a fundraiser in which there are a number of religions present." He said, "Well what should I do about it?"

I said, "Have somebody give a benediction that is not Catholic or not Christian." He said, "Good, you give the benediction." I said, "Ted, there are thirteen senators in this room, I'm not giving a benediction." He said, "We'll go find somebody."

So I went to Senator Frank Lautenberg and I said, "Will you give the benediction?"

He said, "Nancy, I haven't said a prayer since I was in Hebrew school." I said, "Well fine, you've got to say the benediction because I've made a big issue about this." So he gave the benediction, explaining that he was ill-prepared to do it.

Then Ted closed the dinner by saying, "The Catholics gave the invocation and a Jewish member of the Senate gave the benediction. I'm here to apologize to the Protestants."

I'm Not a Puppet

Peter Fenn

Following the 1976 presidential campaign I was working for Senator Frank Church in Washington, DC. I'm still fairly young and trying to do everything I think a staffer is supposed to do.

The Senator and I were walking from his office over to the Senate floor in the Capitol. This was a period of time when staff was increasing and mail was beginning to pour in to congressional offices. It was the late 1970s and things were beginning to change technologically. So I was able to get the list of upcoming legislation and votes from our legislative director.

Instead of using the underground subway between the Senate offices and the Capitol, Church decides he wants to walk outside since it was such a beautiful day.

We're walking down the street and I'm reading him everything I have on upcoming Senate business. Church stops in the middle of my rather lengthy explanation of legislation and scheduled votes and starts acting like a marionette with a puppeteer pulling the strings.

He's right in the middle of the street and people looking over recognize him and start laughing.

Church says, "You guys just constantly pull my strings and tell me what to do like I'm some sort of puppet. You know Peter, I've been around for twenty-four years. I think I can figure out how to vote on my own."

I said, "Senator, I'm sorry. I was just trying to make sure."

He said, "No offense taken."

But it was hilarious. He did a pretty good imitation of a marionette.

Rendon, I Got Other Plans

John Rendon

Immediately after the general election in 1980 when Jimmy Carter lost to Ronald Reagan, the Democratic Party begins looking for a new National Party Chairman. The chairman at the time was John White of Texas.

Bill Clinton had just lost the governorship of Arkansas (by roughly 32,000 votes). He's in Washington, DC, working out of one of the many law firms making phone calls, seeing people, working the present, and thinking about the future.

So I go to see him in my capacity as former Executive Director of the Democratic Party and as a friend. I sit down with him and ask, "So what's going on? There are a lot of people in the party who think we have to move to the middle and we need a young, charismatic guy to be the next party chairman. There are a lot of people who think that you'd make a great National Party Chairman."

Clinton puts down his pen and smiles. He looks at me and says, "Rendon, I got other plans."

He certainly did.

A Moment with the President

Jerry Austin

Because of my experience with African American candidates, such as Jesse Jackson and Carol Moseley Braun, the chairman of the Cook County Democratic Party, Tom Lyons, asked me to write a radio ad for the African American community featuring President Clinton. It was the 1998 midterm election in the wake of the Monica Lewinsky scandal.

The president would be in Chicago later that week to appear at a fundraiser for the Democrats' nominee for governor, former Congressman Glenn Poshard. I wrote a draft of the ad and it was faxed to the political office at the White House. I was told to appear at the fundraiser with an engineer ready to record the president.

I arrived with my engineer in tow. We waited in a holding area until the president finished posing for pictures with Poshard's campaign contributors. Then he walked in to the holding room and greeted me with "Hey man." I started to laugh. Babe Ruth was famous for calling everyone "kid" because he never remembered anyone's name. I had just seen the film *Primary Colors*, where the first time you see John Travolta, playing the Clintonesque character, speak, he says, "Hey man."

The president was led to a small desk and my engineer wired him up for the taping.

The president's aide told me they had rewritten the script because it was too long. My first reaction to reading the new script was, "It's too long and does not focus on the right message to the targeted community in Chicago."

I said nothing. The president did one take. The aide said, "Make it work." A radio ad is usually 60 seconds. The president's one take was 120 seconds.

The president was in a good mood. He asked where he knew me from. I responded that we had met when I ran Jesse Jackson's campaign in 1988 and that I had run Dick Celeste's successful campaigns for governor of Ohio.

The president asked, "How's Celeste doing?"

I thought, he works for you—he's your ambassador to India—why are you asking me? But I responded, "You sent him over there and they dropped the bomb." The president laughed.

As he was exiting, the president predicted to Tom Lyons and me that the Democrats were close to winning back the Congress in next month's election.

I turned to Lyons and said, "This man's delusional."

But in November, the president was almost prophetic: the Democrats won far more congressional seats than expected, despite the Lewinsky scandal.

Bananas

Richard Norman

In 1982, I was managing the congressional campaign for John Wilkerson in South Carolina. He was running in the 5th district, which is the north-central part of the state.

The legendary South Carolina Republican Senator, Strom Thurmond, was a very good friend of the candidate, going back decades. In fact it was Strom who persuaded Wilkerson to run for Congress. He told Wilkerson that if he decided to run, "I'll help you in any way I can." And Strom kept his word—he was very helpful, he went around the district talking to people and raising money for us.

Strom was a very interesting and unique *character*. One of his character traits was his obsession with health food and fitness. He was a fanatic about working out and eating bananas every afternoon around four o'clock.

Anybody who was working with him or spending time with him in the afternoon knew that they had to have bananas handy because he would ask for them.

One afternoon he was making phone calls at the candidate's house. I had asked the candidate's wife beforehand to "make sure that we have some good ripe bananas" there for him to eat—I was certain that around four o'clock he would ask for a banana.

So on this particular day he's making fundraising calls and sure enough it gets to be about four o'clock and he puts down the phone after making just one call and says, "Sonny, I need a banana." He always called me *Sonny*. I said, "Yes sir," and I went into the next room and got him a banana.

He sat there and peeled that banana like he was a little monkey and then ate the whole thing in about five seconds. It was so comical watching him eat that banana that I could barely contain my laughter.

He then proceeded to give me a lecture on nutrition, telling me how important it is to have potassium in the afternoon.

He said, "I eat a banana every afternoon because it's the best form of PO-TAS-SIUM you can get."

From that point on, the candidate and I always took bananas with us when we were campaigning with Strom in the afternoon. Because no matter where we were or what we were doing, he needed his banana at four o'clock and we wanted to be ready.

Airport Security

Steve Cobble

I traveled off and on with Reverend Jackson during the 1990s, as airport security became more of a national presence. This was prior to the September 11 terrorist attack on the World Trade Center, so airport security was not the presence it is today.

Jesse had a well-known habit of getting to the airport late and then hurrying to make his flights. This was always a headache for those traveling with him, because it meant that there would be no space in the overheads by the time we got there, and we would be running through airports, a problem for those of us carrying too many bags (including some of his stuff).

And we invariably ran into tougher security than he did, since he was recognizable all over the planet by this time, especially to the security guards, most of who were African Americans.

Plus Jesse had this habit of just waving to the guards while walking through the exit security when we came to the gate, where everyone would shake hands, kiss his cheek, and let him walk right through. This did not apply to the traveling contingent, so we were left way behind in line, trying to talk our way to the front, as the departure loomed.

One afternoon in Washington, DC's National Airport (never the Reagan Airport, as far as we were concerned), we were running behind and Jesse decided to take the shortcut through the exit security gate. This time the African American guard had his back turned to the exit, facing towards those coming from the gate, as he should have.

Suddenly, over his shoulder behind him, the guard detected movement going the wrong way through the exit, and whirled around, gun drawn.

Jesse raised his hands, big grin on his face, saying, "Don't shoot me, brother!"

I had a clear view of the guard's face, which first registered shock, then a wild grin, as he whirled back to the other (African American) staff working at the security stop.

He kept shouting, "I almost shot Jesse Jackson! I almost shot Jesse!" over and over. The tension broke, everybody breathed a sigh of relief and started laughing.

Two Double Beds

Garry South

All candidates seem to have some kind of *"bizarre candidate habits"* that emerge in the course of the campaign.

My candidate in the 1978 Senate race in Illinois, Alex Seith, had his own peculiar demand. Illinois is a large state and we had to travel a lot in downstate Illinois, sometimes going from small town to small town campaigning.

When Alex was on the road, he always demanded a room with two double beds—nothing else would do, he always insisted on two double beds.

During the general election, we were traveling in southern Illinois and we stopped at a Holiday Inn for the night.

The scheduler that I had hired was instructed by the candidate, in very colorful and profane language, that he never wanted to walk into a hotel or motel room that did not have two double beds. That was his only real demand but he was adamant about it. Every room he stayed in had to have two—not one—double beds.

So we arrive at this Holiday Inn in yet one more small town in southern Illinois. I remember they had one of those old electric signs outside with the arrow coming out pointing back to the motel. One of those signs that had messages like, *"Welcome and Congratulations to the Graduating Class of 1978."*

It was apparently rare for statewide candidates to visit this little hamlet, and having Seith visit and stay there overnight was a big deal. So at this particular Holiday Inn the message on the sign that night was *"Welcome Alex Seith."* We enter the lobby and it's late, around two o'clock in the morning. The desk clerk is waiting for us and all primed for our arrival.

She greets us and is obviously excited that the candidate has finally arrived. She says, "Oh, welcome, Mr. Seith, we've been expecting you, we're so happy to have you here today. Thank you for deciding to stay at our Holiday Inn. To make your stay more comfortable, we have upgraded you free of charge to a suite with a king-size bed!"

You would have thought she had just told him he would be sleeping on the floor in a closet because he goes completely bananas.

Seith starts yelling at the desk clerk, "I don't want a king-size bed, I ordered two double beds, didn't my scheduler tell you? Give me that phone!" He grabs the phone out of her hands and punches "o" for the hotel operator.

This poor clerk is stunned and the look on her face was like, "What is going on here?" I'm sure the look on my face mirrored the expression on hers.

So at two o'clock in the morning, Seith calls our scheduler back in Chicago, gets her out of bed, and orders her to get on the phone with the desk clerk and confirm that she had reserved a room with two double beds.

The scheduler, of course, has no idea what is going on, and is pissed that she's just been roused out of a sound sleep. "Alex," she says, "Is there a problem with the reservation or something?"

Seith starts screaming at her, "YES, there's something wrong with the reservation! You know I said two double beds, not one bed, not a king-size bed—TWO DOUBLE BEDS!"

The scheduler is now totally flustered and upset. "Alex, I told them you needed a room with two double beds. It's obviously just a mistake, the hotel probably upgraded you for free. Plus, why are you calling me in the middle of the night, you're standing right there at the front desk, take care of it yourself!"

The candidate's voice gets even louder. "I don't care if it's the middle of the night! I want TWO double beds! Get on the phone with this lady right now and fix it!"

The totally befuddled clerk, in an effort to diffuse the situation, puts on her friendliest smile and says, "No problem, sir, let me see if we have a room with two double beds."

It was utterly bizarre. None of us ever knew why he had to have two double beds. We did, however, speculate and develop our own theories.

He would never let anybody in his room. When you came to pick him up, he never let you enter his room. Most candidates would say something like "Yeah, come on in, I'm still shaving."

But Seith would always insist you wait outside the door and when he was ready he would come out.

Our theory was that he had some obsessive-compulsive disorder and had to lay out his clothes for the next day on the second bed or he couldn't function.

That was *our theory,* but of course, no one ever knew for sure why he insisted on two double beds.

Celebrity for a Day

Jerry Austin

In the 1972 McGovern presidential campaign, I was the co-coordinator of the 23rd Congressional District in Ohio. After the national convention, one of my initial assignments was to open neighborhood offices throughout the congressional district.

I requested a celebrity for a day to open the offices and attract the media.

My request was granted and I was told my celebrity would be former Senator from Ohio, Stephen Young. Young had retired in 1970 and was known as an early opponent of the Vietnam war as well as a lifelong maverick. He was also very short and very old, aged 82.

I sent one of my young staffers to pick him up at the airport and gave him my 1968 Impala with a dent in the fender to use as the campaign limo.

At the first stop, a nice crowd had gathered and a newspaper reporter and one television station were also present.

The master of ceremonies was the local state representative. When Young arrived, I was at the curbside to open the door. He was seated in the back seat. My staffer was in the driver's seat and the Senator was seated in the rear seat as if he were riding in a limo or taxi. I looked at the young staffer and he just rolled his eyes. I asked if he had briefed the Senator and he responded, "Yes, but he did not seem to be paying attention."

Young walked in to the storefront headquarters as he was being introduced by the emcee. After the modest applause died down, Young began to speak.

He said, "At my age sex is not very frequent." I could not believe my ears or my eyes. Young continued, "I am over eighty and I realize my best sexual years are behind me." I quickly grabbed the emcee and told him to get the microphone away from Young and thank him and end the program.

As I ushered Young out to the curb, I told the staffer to take him back to the hotel and drop him off. He was scheduled to stay overnight and we would make sure he was driven to the airport the next day.

It was obvious that the Senator was borderline senile or was suffering from Alzheimer's.

The staffer drove him to the hotel. Young, again, sat in the back seat. At the hotel as he opened the rear door for Young, the Senator asked, "Young man—wait here for me while I freshen up. I'll be back in a few minutes and then you can join me for dinner at my favorite Cleveland restaurant."

Young departed the car and entered the hotel. When Young was out of sight the staffer found a public phone and called me to ask, "What do I do?" I said, "Wait for him and take him to eat. You'll get a good free meal."

A number of hours passed. I was at home when the doorbell rang and it was the staffer who came by to return my car. I asked, "Where did you eat?" He reported that Young came down from his hotel room two hours later after the staffer had called the room to remind him he was waiting downstairs. Young, again, entered the car through the rear door and proceeded to direct the driver towards "his favorite restaurant in Cleveland."

After a ten-minute drive, the Senator exclaimed, "There, there it is—turn in here." It was a hamburger drive-in. I laughed and asked, "How was the burger?" He said, "Best I've ever had." I responded, "Good, then you'll drive the Senator to the airport the next morning. And use your own car."

The next day the driver arrived in his 1969 beaten-up Toyota. Young, again, entered, although not through the rear door. This was a two-door. He pulled the front seat toward him and sat in the back seat.

A Pizza Guy

John Toohey

The most difficult trip I ever advanced was a trip to Brussels with Vice President Al Gore. I love Brussels, but this was a real challenging trip.

We had all the time in the world for Gore's trip, but things just got out of control within our team due to a lack of discipline. As a result, I ended up doing something in front of Gore that I probably shouldn't have.

First there was an incident between me and the Secret Service that caused some friction. I wasn't even lead advance, but the guy who was lead was a close friend. He wasn't in charge of his team like he should have been. It wasn't all his fault. But we ended up doing way more work than we should have.

That's the nature of the beast, there are a lot of moving parts, and there are a lot of people with different opinions and you have to try to make everyone happy.

In Brussels we had to move Gore through two public events that were located in very large, spacious sites, and both events were very complex.

One was a technology exhibition that interested Gore. We knew that the site person there was an idiot and he wasn't going to be able to handle it. So I took on most of the advance work on that one and the lead for the advance team, Patrick, became a site person too, which he shouldn't have had to do. We were overextended. It was a really stressful day for us and it was the one and only time that I laid hands on a fellow team member in a threatening way.

It was just one of those things that got out of control. This kid on the team was pulling on my sleeve and nothing was working the way it should be. No control anywhere. Without the Secret Service we probably would have been overrun because this kid, who was supposed to be advancing the trip, had done nothing for ten days.

It wasn't so much what I said in front of Gore but what I did. We were overwhelmed as it was, trying to keep everything running smoothly. And this kid keeps tugging on my sleeve to get my attention. I'm trying to go this way and trying to go that way, with way too much to do. And this kid just keeps tugging at me—"Hey, Toohey…hey, Toohey."

Finally I spun around and grabbed him by the lapels. He was a guy from Boston, and I just ran him into a corner. I told him to just shut up, "just shut up and don't move. If you move, I'm going to hurt you. If you move from this corner, I swear, I'm going to hurt you. You understand?" He nodded.

Obviously Gore saw what was going on and he turns to the Secret Service and says, "I don't know what's going on over there, but I think Toohey is a little pissed off at that guy. Who is he?"

The response was, "It's all right sir. I think it was just a pizza guy. Now, if you're ready, let's keep going."

The "pizza guy" never moved from that corner.

Saturday Night Live
Steve Cobble

In the early 1990s, Frank Watkins went with Jesse Jackson to New York City for his appearance on *Saturday Night Live* (*SNL*). *SNL* was doing a skit honoring a Dr. Seuss anniversary. But neither one of them had ever read the Dr. Seuss story, *Green Eggs and Ham*, which Jesse was supposed to read live on the *SNL* news segment that night.

My memory of the story, which Frank told me, was that Jackson took a nap during the first part of the show. The news segment was on late, most often coming on after midnight. Jesse had not been in New York earlier in the week, so he had not done a run-through with the cast.

About ten minutes before he was due on stage, the celebrity guest, who I thought was Michael Jordan, but Frank said recently was Spike Lee, came in to the dressing room backstage, quite worried, wondering if Jesse should be awakened to get ready for his appearance.

Frank was not concerned. He was used to Jesse's naps, his ability to wake up and hit his stride immediately. Right before show time, Jesse did wake up, looked at Frank and said, "Okay, where's the book?"

"I thought you had it."

"No, I gave it to you."

"I don't have it."

"Well, I don't have it."

The end result was that neither one could find the book. *SNL*, however, prepares for such problems, and one of the crew ran off, and hustled back with a spare copy, just as the announcer was bringing Jesse on stage.

Without missing a step, Jesse took the book, walked out, and blew everyone in the studio and TV audiences away with the greatest live reading of Dr. Seuss *ever*.

"I do not like them, Sam I Am.

I do not like green eggs and ham."

I had not known Jesse was going to be on *SNL* that night. My wife Molly and I were just watching it as we often did. When he came on and read that story in his preacher role, I about fell off the couch laughing—it was one of the most hilarious skits ever!

Mosquito Inspector

Steve Murphy

My career began with Jimmy Carter's 1976 presidential campaign.

In 1975, I had been following the articles about Jimmy Carter that Johnny Apple was writing in the *New York Times*, including a really glowing *Sunday Times Magazine* article. In December, I run into a fellow Vista volunteer at a Christmas party. He said, "Hey, do you want to go to Mississippi for Jimmy Carter? A friend of a friend is looking for organizers to work with the state director."

I said yes and ended up doing the interview over the phone. Basically, I embellished my organizing experience so that every two hours that I had done something on an election day became two months. I just flat-out lied to the guy.

But I got hired and was sent to Natchez. I had three counties. I did well in my counties, and I was the first person in the Carter Campaign to solicit a thousand-dollar contribution other than Jimmy Carter. I actually got somebody who had never met Jimmy Carter to give us a thousand dollars.

Mississippi was a caucus state. It was after Iowa, but before New Hampshire. The caucuses were really exciting because it was the first time that the two Democratic parties in the state—the regular Democratic Party (segregationist) and the Freedom Democratic Party (integrationist)—caucused together. There was a lot of trepidation about what would happen.

Basically the plan was to get African American voters to the caucuses. George Wallace won the caucus but I did considerably better in my area because it's not like the Bible Belt—the conservative, white, evangelical—part of the state.

The day after the caucuses a group of us went to meet with Hamilton Jordan, who was in Mississippi for the weekend. We wanted to know if the national campaign would hire some of us as organizers. I had to type up a resumé and I didn't even know what a resumé was—or how to type. I put everything on that resumé that I could think of, including helping in my grandfather's warehouse in the summer, my volunteer work with Vista, and a summer job I had as a junior mosquito inspector.

I hand the resumé to Hamilton Jordan. He looks it over and says, "Look, you did a little better over your way in Natchez and you're the first person other than Jimmy Carter in this entire campaign to get a thousand dollars out of anybody. But I'm going to hire you and put you on the campaign because you were a mosquito inspector and I was a mosquito inspector too."

So I'm in this business today because Hamilton Jordan and I had both been mosquito inspectors.

Are You from New Orleans?

Tom King

In 1979, a friend of mine from Boston called me up and said, "Hey, they're looking for somebody to go and organize some of the unions down in Louisiana. Are you interested?" I said "Sure."

I fly down to Louisiana and meet with the manager for the campaign for Louis Landon—they used to call him "Lying Louie Landon."

I was sent to Shreveport, which hadn't seen union organizing in years. We're doing this big union event and there were about two hundred people who showed up. We start getting them organized into teams to knock on doors and distribute literature. I give them my big rah-rah, "we can do this" speech.

A guy comes up to me afterwards; he was about six foot, six inches tall—really big guy. He's looking down on me and I'm not short at about six foot four.

He's looking at me, checking me out, trying to figure out where I'm from, and he says, "Boy, you talk funny."

I thought, "Oh, here it comes. I'm an outsider, a carpetbagger." I mean, my accent is pure Boston!

He repeated, "Boy, you talk *real* funny."

I was thinking he's about to launch in to, "you Yankee no good son of a—"

Instead he says, "Are you from New Orleans?"

So I just said yes and walked away.

From that day forward, anytime I'm anywhere in the south I tell everybody I'm from New Orleans.

Jamillah

Jerry Austin

Jamillah Muhammed was an aide to Jackie Jackson, wife of the Reverend Jesse Jackson during his 1988 campaign for the Democratic Party presidential nomination.

I recruited Jamillah to join the campaign and assigned her to the toughest congressional district in the country.

In Louisiana during the Super Tuesday primary, she located thousands of Jackson brochures in the garage of our state coordinator. She confronted the coordinator asking why these brochures weren't at the campaign headquarters instead. He responded by yelling at her, telling her to get out of Louisiana.

She responded, "I only take orders from three people—Jesus, Jesse, and Jerry."

The coordinator replied, "Who's Jerry?"

Jenrette

Jerry Austin

John Jenrette was a longtime Democratic Congressman from the Myrtle Beach area of South Carolina. He had been arrested in the ABSCAM investigation, where FBI agents ran a sting operation against members of Congress.

I received a call from a friend in South Carolina who asked that I meet with Jenrette to help him plan a comeback. I thought he was still in jail. When I was informed that he served his time and was back home, I agreed to meet with him.

Jenrette met me at the airport. He was handsome, articulate, and very bright. We talked for awhile and he told me he loved serving in Congress and wanted to return. I told him a return to Congress was a long shot but he needed to raise money for a poll to learn whether he was on a suicide mission.

I accompanied him on several visits to old contributors. They were all very gracious and encouraged him to run. Almost all took me to the side and said that they owed him, but did not believe that a comeback was in the cards.

Before I left, I told him there was something I had to ask. I wanted to know what was his state of mind when he was stung by the FBI.

He had walked into a hotel room in Washington and met with two men who were wearing a bed sheet wrapped around their heads and sunglasses over their eyes. "Didn't you know this was a setup?" I asked. He responded, "They knew how to pick their targets. I was into drugs and needed money. If those two men were naked it wouldn't have made any difference. I was going to make some money—that was all that was important."

I arranged for the poll to be conducted. The results were not encouraging and he decided not to run. The last I heard of John Jenrette involved his arrest for shoplifting a pair of shoes from a local discount store.

Humble Pie Act

Garry South

When I was working for Dick Celeste we would fly overseas quite a bit, and I went with him on some of the trips to Asia. Typically we would have our head of security, Lieutenant Strine, with us.

The routine was always the same, whatever airline we were flying, whether it was Delta or a foreign airline. Strine would go to the customer service rep at the airport and say, "We have the Governor of Ohio on the flight today," and generally speaking they would usually upgrade him to first class.

Under Ohio law, we could book business class but we couldn't book first class, so he would book business class and anyone traveling with him would also be booked in business class.

In California it's against the law for a public official to get upgraded—it's a felony offense because it constitutes an illegal gift. But not in Ohio: in Ohio it was legal to accept an upgrade.

The first couple of times we went overseas this worked like a charm. Strine would inform them that the governor would be on the flight and when Dick got to the counter they would gush.

"Oh Governor, we're so happy to have you on our flight today. We'd like to upgrade you to first class."

And Celeste would play the whole "humble pie" act, saying, "Oh, you don't have to do that—I'm perfectly happy in business class—I'm sure there's plenty of leg room there. It's totally unnecessary. You really don't have to do that—totally unnecessary. I appreciate it, but—" *and then he'd accept the upgrade.*

One time we were flying Japan Air Lines (JAL) from Columbus to Seattle and changing planes in Seattle.

When we get to Seattle, Strine does his usual routine with the JAL customer service rep, then returns to the governor and says, "I'm sorry Governor but they can't upgrade you to first class because first class is *completely, totally* booked."

And Celeste erupts! "What the hell? I'm the *Governor* of *Ohio*, what do they think…"

The "humble pie" act dropped off the radar screen.

Winning the Nose Ring Vote

Steve Cobble

The 1984 Democratic National Convention was in San Francisco. I attended as an aide/speechwriter for New Mexico Governor Toney Anaya. I had the honor of working on his convention seconding speech for Vice-Presidential nominee Geraldine Ferraro.

My friend Jan Hartke, son of the former Senator from Indiana, Vance Hartke, and one of the funniest people I have ever met in politics, was also there as an Anaya advisor.

Earlier that year, the very progressive *Mother Jones* magazine had contacted the governor's office in Santa Fe about the possibility of naming Toney Anaya as America's most progressive governor.

Since I was the aide in the office assumed most likely to have actually read *Mother Jones*—a correct assumption—I was given the job of filling out the nomination form.

Whether that helped or not, Governor Anaya was indeed named as the country's most progressive governor, and we were invited to an event in San Francisco during convention week to honor him and other progressive champions, including Jim Hightower, at that time head of the Texas Agriculture Department. Since I had filled out the nomination form everyone in Anaya's office associated me with the *Mother Jones* award.

By July of 1984, Governor Anaya was hurting in the opinion polls in New Mexico, due largely to his political bravery in pushing through a needed tax the year before. And New Mexico in 1984 was not a cutting-edge state, culturally. So even though cities like Santa Fe and Taos had liberal subcultures, the state as a whole was still very traditional, heavily Catholic, and culturally conservative.

Jan and I arrived early at the restaurant/bar where the *Mother Jones* celebration was to be held and knocked on the door. A very pleasant young woman opened it, and guided us up to the chosen room. But her pleasantness was not what registered immediately to us. What caught our eye was her purple hair—or maybe it was her prominent nose ring.

Think back to 1984. Purple hair and nose rings were not standard props in New Mexico politics three decades ago, and this was a governor from that culturally conservative state getting an award from a "Bay Area," left-leaning magazine.

Jan immediately started in on me. "Oh great, Cobble, way to go! This is really going to help us in the polls in Roswell now. Purple hair. Nose rings. We'll just dominate the art scene vote in Santa Fe, while sacrificing every vote in Carlsbad and Socorro and Silver City. Good thing we're getting the *Mother Jones* award. Good move on your part—"

We could not stop laughing. The truth is, Jan was proud his governor was the most progressive in the country and glad *Mother Jones* had recognized him for it.

But the culture clash was just too obvious to ignore, and the ribbing continued the rest of the week as my great political thinking that had just secured the purple hair/nose ring voting base for Governor Anaya.

A Scary Invitation

Jerry Austin

During the 1988 Democratic Presidential Primary in California, I was introduced to one of Reverend Jackson's longtime supporters, the disc jockey Casey Kasem.

Casey was originally from Detroit and was very active in developing a dialogue between Israeli and Palestinian groups in the Los Angeles area.

In the 1984 Jackson campaign, Casey hosted a fairly successful fundraiser and was asked to do the same in 1988. Casey and his actress wife Jean lived in a penthouse apartment atop a luxury hotel.

I met with them to help plan their event. They wanted the event to raise money but also wanted to make sure it was fun. They had secured Wolfgang Puck's Spago restaurant for a Sunday afternoon event. They chose a western theme with the invited guests asked to dress as cowboys and cowgirls.

The additional special touch was to have the invitations delivered by messenger. The invitation would be enclosed in a box with a chocolate cowboy hat and boot.

A week before the event, the invitations began to arrive. I received a call from Jean who was panicked to learn that the hand-delivered invitation had met with a disastrous result.

Many of the invitees were Palestinian and Israeli activists. When a messenger tried to deliver the box to one of the activist invitees, the potential recipient was suspicious and called the bomb squad. The messenger did not know what was in the box. The bomb squad arrived. They proceeded to use their special equipment to carefully open the box.

When it was discovered that the potential bomb was a chocolate cowboy hat and boot, the invitee was relieved and embarrassed. This same scenario occurred with three separate invitees and an item appeared in the local paper.

IV. Leadership and Appreciation

Remembering Mo

Karen T. Scates

Working for Mo Udall, the former Democratic Congressman from Arizona, was one of the great privileges of my life. He was a great public servant, an amazing orator, a committed environmentalist, and a valued friend of Democrats and Republicans. His most distinguishing characteristic was his personality. He was unimpressed by the self-important phonies in politics and had the amazing and unique gift of humor. One of his favorite sayings was, "Flattery is OK, if you don't inhale!"

With Mo's rare combination of attributes, it was a wonderful and challenging experience working for him. Usually the staff provides the expertise and support to elevate their boss, but with Mo, it was a stretch to be as good as he was in style and substance. You were trying to always live up to the values and principles that he lived by.

He was very loyal to his staff, although he didn't really get involved in your personal life, he didn't ask you how your kids were doing or how your family was. On a personal level he didn't engage. He didn't know where you went at night when you went home. I don't know if it ever concerned him or if he even wondered.

I remember a few of us, staffers primarily, would work late into the night coming up with new plans and ways that he could become president. We wondered if he even knew that we were going to those extremes, spending our evenings figuring out how we were going to make the world a better place and do it with him.

He was a very deep thinker and he had a strong moral center. As a result he saw the world in a particular way based on what *he* thought was the right thing to do for future generations. A historical example was his famous floor speech against the Vietnam War, when he could no longer keep silent, and broke ranks with the leader of his own Democratic Party, President Lyndon Johnson.

After running for the Democratic presidential nomination in 1976, Mo faced a restless constituency in Tucson, largely because they felt neglected while he was away from his home district. His reelection in 1978 was very close. The Republican National Committee worked overtime to defeat him. In an example of how his honesty and public engagement almost backfired, he took on the needed reform of the 1872 Mining Law. The powerful mining interests ganged up on him and accused him of being a socialist and printed his voting record on "pink" paper.

Mo didn't stoop to those tactics and he won the election. In many ways it was an example of how he succeeded and proved that a heated contest could be won with honor, civility, tenacity, humor, and commitment to principle. He believed in a continuing dialogue between citizens and their leaders.

Mo wasn't entirely comfortable on a one-on-one basis, especially around women. He enjoyed being around guys and liked to throw out one-liners and tell jokes. He really lit up in front of large groups of people. He would amuse himself with the jokes he always told, although sometimes they were totally inappropriate.

One time he was getting an honorarium. He was speaking in a synagogue and it was packed. There were thousands of people and someone plopped a yarmulke on his head and it was sort of cock-eyed sideways and I guess he thought that was the way you were supposed to wear it because he didn't fix it.

Everybody had something to say: Golda Meir this, Golda Meir that. It was 1979 and Golda Meir had just died a few months before so she was the topic of every conversation. I could see that Mo was thinking "What am I doing here? What am I going to say to this audience about Golda Meir?"

I'm thinking this is not going to go well.

So Mo gets up and says, "You know I feel just terrible about Golda Meir, she was a great leader. But I am reminded of a story."

My reaction was "Oh no."

And, sure enough, Mo proceeds to tell what could be seen as an anti-Semitic joke and it did not go over very well.

The joke went something like this:

"Golda Meir was asked how it was that the Israelis were so successful at winning wars. Israel is the size of the state of New Jersey and they are surrounded by all these enemies. What is it that you do or that you know that helps you win? Can you give us your secret?"

"So Golda Meir says: Oh yes, we dig three trenches and in the first trench we put a row of lawyers, in the second trench we put a row of lawyers, and in the third trench we put a row of dentists. Then someone yells charge and boy, do they know how to charge—"

This was not the ideal joke to tell in a synagogue, right on the heels of the death of Golda Meir. Half the audience was probably confused as to why he told it and the other half were probably offended.

It was the same thing when the Polish Pope was appointed—he was going around telling Polish jokes.

I had Mo in this rural community and he was on the radio station telling a Polish joke about the new Pope!

Afterwards I suggested that it might not be appropriate to tell Polish jokes about the new Pope. Challenging Mo about one of his jokes was not an easy thing to do. He sort of listened to me and the next time he got up in front of a group he told another Polish Pope joke!

Meeting Ronald Reagan

Bill Lacy

I first became interested in politics when I was in high school. I remember the very first thing I did politically was asking my dad to take me down to the Republican headquarters in 1964 to pick up a Goldwater bumper strip when I was just ten years old. He refused to do it because he had political ambitions as a Democrat and didn't want to be seen stopping off at Republican headquarters.

My mom was from a Republican family and ended up taking me—there was a bit of a split in the family when it came to politics.

When I entered college, I got involved with Young Americans for Freedom, which would probably be a similar refrain for a lot of guys like me. And we quickly found out that we could make a difference. At Vanderbilt, like a lot of universities back in the early 1970s, the student senate was very liberal and they were bringing in all these *very* liberal speakers.

So a group of us who were conservative Republicans started protesting. We would protest the speakers who were coming by putting a table out at the student union and talking to other students about how unfair it was that all the speakers coming in were liberals.

Finally the student senate came to us and said, "Who would *you* like to have come in and speak?" Basically they were throwing us a bone to get us off their backs so they would look like they were balancing out the speakers.

A bunch of us got together and decided to see if we could get Ronald Reagan, who had just finished his term as governor of California, to come in and speak.

That's how I first met Ronald Reagan: he agreed to come speak at Vanderbilt. That's also how I first got to know Mike Deaver, who came with him.

As part of his visit the student senate put together a dinner for a group of students which included both conservatives and liberals; and we all got to meet and spend time with Reagan.

So we found out pretty early on that we could make a difference—a small group of dedicated people who were passionate about an idea.

This was obviously before Reagan ran for president but even then he was extraordinarily impressive. The thing that stunned me at the time was that although he was sitting there with a group of both liberals and conservatives, he seemed genuinely interested in what *all* the students had to say—the liberals as well as the conservatives.

That was a real eye-opener for us. For me, it was probably my first experience with the notion that you should respect the other side—even though we kind of felt that way anyway.

Today that's a different way of looking at politics, but I believe that although you may be a Democrat or you may be a Republican, so what? It doesn't really matter when it comes to respect and civility.

Ted's Humanity

Nancy Korman

When I first got involved in politics, you didn't need to be rich to have a role. You just needed to be energetic. That's what made it so much fun.

I was living in Newton, Massachusetts, when I got to know Ted Kennedy. I had attended a fundraiser for Michael Harrington, who was a Congressman from the North Shore. I had parked my car at the bottom of a hill to walk to the event, but I encountered a bunch of people protesting and blocking the pathway to the fundraiser.

They were furious because Kennedy was going to be speaking. He was against the Hyde Amendment, which meant he was "pro-abortion." He also wasn't taking a stand against busing, so the conservatives were furious with him.

The protestors came armed with tomatoes and eggs which they planned on throwing at Kennedy. I parked my car next to the space reserved for Ted Kennedy. When I got out of the car they thought the Senator had arrived and pelted *me* with the tomatoes and eggs.

When Kennedy arrived, he was mortified that this nice young woman was covered with tomatoes and eggs.

I told him, "Don't worry about it. It's just the first time a Jewish girl felt like Joan of Arc."

He chuckled and sent me flowers with an apology the next day. I phoned him and said, "You didn't need to send me flowers Senator, but I am so mad at those protestors that I decided to host a fundraiser for you at my house."

I had the fundraiser at my house for a donation of $100 to his Senate campaign. I introduced him at the event since I was the host.

"Senator, before I introduce you to the people in this room, I want to introduce the people in this room to you. These people are from the Catholic Interracial Council. They are people who support fair housing; they represent organizations that promote civil rights, human rights, women's rights. I'd like you to know that for the people in this room, you are a lot more than just a piece of Camelot."

From that day forward Ted Kennedy and I were friends. He wrote to me and I wrote back to him, every month after that day, from 1974 until he died. Since I didn't need a job and didn't want to work professionally on a campaign, I could say whatever I wished.

He was a multifaceted person who certainly had his flaws as a human being. But he was also a very, very good person. He was good in a profound kind of way.

When I say that, people always ask, "Well what about Chappaquiddick?" And I tell them, "Nobody goes through life without mistakes and without horrible situations."

I'm not minimizing what happened or cancelling that out. But you have to also consider the rest of his life. He took time out of his schedule to volunteer as a reader in public school. His entire time in the United States Senate, every Tuesday, he went and read to some first grader. He did the real work of humanity. I never forgot that.

The Nuclear Codes

Richard Norman

Senator Strom Thurmond of South Carolina was a member of The Sporting Club, a gym in Virginia. He would go there and swim in the pool every afternoon. He was an amazing swimmer. He was in tremendous shape and this was when he was in his eighties. I would come in and he would be in the pool, so I would go into the gym and work out for about an hour or so and then come back out to the pool area and he's still swimming laps.

At the gym there is a very big jacuzzi in the men's locker room that could easily seat twenty-five guys. There were always a lot of people in the gym because it was a really large facility. Strom would always come in and sit in the jacuzzi after he was done swimming.

One day when I was in the men's locker room Strom came in and got into the Jacuzzi. I said hello and he acknowledged me. And I asked him, "Who are your friends here?" Because he had two big guys in dark suits standing behind him protectively and both had a communications device in their ear.

Strom said, "Sonny, those are the United States Secret Service. The President of the United States is under anesthesia and the Vice President of the United States is out of the country and I am the President pro tem of the Senate."

"As President pro tem of the Senate, I am now the acting President of the United States and those gentlemen over there have the codes to the nuclear arsenal."

Jokingly, I said, "Sir I hope we don't get into any situation where you would have to use those," and he just responded, "I hope so too Sonny."

It was amazing that he just took the whole thing in stride. He was now in charge of the nuclear codes but it didn't affect him at all and certainly didn't disrupt his fitness routine because he was a fanatic when it came to fitness and health.

The First Catholic Priest in Congress

Nancy Korman

In the 1970s, if you lived in a big old house, which I did, and you were willing to put in sweat equity, which I was, you could get involved in politics.

Back then people didn't give thousands of dollars, there were no PACs. You did a barbeque at $25 per person with six cosponsors; one was in charge of the hamburgers, one was in charge of the potato salad, one was in charge of the dessert, and you made a couple of grand and gained some volunteers who then became political activists.

We did it with sweat equity; we didn't do it through big connections. But we did it successfully.

By the early 1970s I had already worked on a number of campaigns when I had my first child. One year in December I threw a holiday party and invited a number of my political activist friends.

Several friends of mine, an activist named Arthur Obermayer and a guy named Jerry Grossman, were standing in my dining room holding buffet plates, and said, "We're going to go down to Boston College and ask Bob Drinan to run for Congress. You want to come with us?"

I immediately said, "I can't come with you, I have a new baby!"

He said, "Well, in order to convince him to run we have to promise him that we have a team in place. So what role can you play in the campaign? What are you going to be?"

I said, "I don't know what I'm going to be, what are *you* going to be?"

Jerry said, "I'll be the campaign chief." Arthur said, "I'll be the campaign treasurer."

I said, "Jerry, are you going to do fundraising?"

He said, "Yes," so I said, "I'll be the vice chair of fundraising."

I figured this wasn't going anywhere because Father Bob Drinan, who was a Catholic priest, was never going to say yes—but he did.

We would have finance committee meetings at my house and Bob Drinan would say at each meeting, "Do not throw trash in the basket, there's a baby in there." My child's first word was not "mama" or "daddy," it was "Bobby," because that's what he kept hearing, Bobby Drinan, Bobby Drinan, Bobby Drinan.

Surprising everyone, Father Robert Drinan, a liberal, antiwar, human rights activist, lawyer, and Roman Catholic Jesuit priest won and became a member of Congress.

Drinan became very popular with liberal activists in the Democratic Party. He filed a resolution in 1973 to impeach Nixon, openly supported abortion rights, and introduced legislation to end the war in Vietnam.

Father Drinan was a fascinating person because he was Roman Catholic but he was a Jesuit, so he was totally focused on scholarly pursuits. You never, ever had this sense that you were buying into liturgy; you were buying into ending the war, you were buying into civil rights, you buying into moral values. So for me, as a Jewish person, and for many of his Jewish supporters, there was no conflict at all.

As a matter of fact, he once teased us at a meeting, telling us "I'm a Jesuit, *but Society of Jesus, SJ,* so for this group, that means *somewhat Jewish.*"

He was a wonderful man; absolutely honest and above board and decent. He influenced many lives during his remarkable time in Congress.

Still Conservative After All These Years

Bill Lacy

I'm a steadfast Republican, but my father was a Democrat. It was 1976 and my dad had run in 1974 and won his district for the state Senate, which consisted of ten counties. All ten counties were entirely within what was then Tennessee's 4th Congressional District held by Congressman Joe L. Evins for thirty years as a conservative Democrat. Then he decided to retire.

The 4th Congressional District was one of those districts where winning the Democratic primary, as V. O. Key once wrote, "was tantamount to election." So everybody started jumping into the Democratic primary for an open seat.

A group of conservatives recruited a guy named T. Tommy Cutrer who was a personality on WSM radio in Nashville. WSM was the home of the Grand Ole Opry. Prior to joining WSM, T. Tommy had been a successful disc jockey and became the announcer for the Grand Ole Opry.

As a candidate, he had several things going for him. He had great name ID, he was politically conservative, and he had this amazing ability to look into the camera and make you think he was talking to you personally.

A group of people had contacted Dad because his ten counties were in the 4th District. So Dad agrees to go to this meeting to talk about the congressional race and he asked me if I wanted to go with him. Now this is two years after his Senate race and I've already learned how to do targeting, ads, budgeting, and all that stuff—at a rudimentary kind of level.

Before the meeting, I did what I always do in politics—because I was always very much into the planning—I put together about ten typewritten pages of notes on things that I thought should be considered by the campaign.

The meeting was basically a group of southern good ole boys who agreed to attend this meeting on a Sunday afternoon at T. Tommy's home. All of them had opinions but none of them, as they would be the first to admit, really knew exactly what they were doing when it came to campaigns.

Finally they got around to asking Dad what he thought and he said, "Well, I think you ought to listen to what my son Bill has to say here because he's brought about ten pages of notes." So I just started outlining my notes and by the end of the session they had hired me as the campaign manager to run T. Tommy's campaign.

I was only about twenty-two years old at the time, and I made it very clear up front that I was a Republican, not a Democrat. I'm a conservative but T. Tommy was *very* conservative—the most conservative guy in the race as it turned out.

We could never really raise any money—we wound up raising around $100,000 to $150,000—and we put virtually all of that into radio and TV ads. We did two classic ads where our candidate was just talking directly into the camera. Nothing fancy at all—literally in a studio talking to the camera.

As I recall there were nine candidates in the race. We knew that there wouldn't be a Republican in the general election so whoever won the primary won the seat. It was winner-take-all regardless of your percentage with no runoff.

We ended up finishing in third place. The guy who finished second was the Speaker of the House in the state of Tennessee, and the guy who won became a U.S. Senator and Vice President—Al Gore.

I got to know Al Gore during the campaign because I ran into him repeatedly on the campaign trail. He actually called me up after he won and offered me a job and I just said, "Well that's very kind of you and I can't even begin to tell you how honored I am that you thought of me, but I'm a conservative Republican. Given this, I don't think that's a good idea for either of us."

I wound up in Washington, DC, a year later and he had a person from his congressional staff come by and visit with me from time to time. I figured they were keeping tabs on me. Or maybe he thought that I was going to change my mind about being a conservative or supporting the Republican Party. But, to this day, I'm still a conservative and proud to be a Republican.

A Job Interview

Jerry Austin

When I became a full time political consultant in 1978, I had a goal to run a presidential campaign in 1988. My candidate would be Dick Celeste. But after being reelected to a second term as Ohio Governor in 1986, Celeste took a look at the potential of his candidacy for President and decided it was not in the cards. Although I had received some recognition for running his two successful campaigns, I did not have a national reputation. I was the Ohio contact—if you wanted to know anything about Ohio, call Jerry Austin.

In September of 1987, I received a phone call from Danny Blakemore, an old friend, an activist, and the first African American president of an investment banking firm. He lived in Los Angeles.

He called and told me he attended a Jesse Jackson for President meeting the previous evening. Then Assemblywoman Maxine Waters presided. Although the purpose of the meeting was to plan a fundraiser for later in the year, a question was asked about the progress of finding a national campaign manager. Maxine reported they were still looking. It was difficult to find a reputable campaign manager because Jackson's 1984 presidential campaign was so helter-skelter. The best campaign managers in the country had signed with other potential candidates.

Danny said, "How about Jerry Austin?" The assembled group almost responded in unison, "Who's this?" Danny answered, "Jerry ran Dick Celeste's two successful campaigns for Governor of Ohio." The group had heard of Celeste and encouraged Danny to call me and inquire about my interest in being Jesse Jackson's national campaign manager.

Danny asked me the question and my response was, "No, I am not interested." He did not give up. "Would you come to California and have lunch with Willie Brown and dinner with Maxine Waters to discuss the campaign?" he queried. I responded, "Of course." The chance to meet Willie Brown, then the Speaker of the California State Assembly, was very inviting. Willie and I had never met, but I was a McGovern supporter in 1972 and was at the convention in Miami when he pleaded to "give me back my delegation."

Over the next fifteen years, Brown had become Speaker and one of the most powerful political leaders in the country. I began my cross-country journey to have lunch with Brown in San Francisco and dinner with Maxine in Los Angeles.

I arrived at Brown's law office and was asked to wait until he finished with a phone call. After a half an hour, Brown came to the lobby area, greeted me and said, "Let's get some lunch." We exited the office and walked to his car, which was parked in front of a fire hydrant. He smiled and said, "One of the perks."

Sitting down at one of his favorite restaurants, he began the conversation by asking, "What makes you think a white guy can run the campaign of Jesse Jackson?" I looked puzzled. I said I did not know if I wanted to run the race but that I was the most qualified white guy for the job. I continued, "Mr. Speaker, I am the most successful political consultant you never heard of." Brown laughed and asked me to tell him about my qualifications.

I began. I grew up in the South Bronx. One third of the neighborhood was black, one third was Puerto Rican, and one third was white. The one-third white was one third Jewish, one third Irish, and one third Italian. My parents both worked. My father worked in the fur industry and my mother worked for a group of Jewish pharmacists who became 1199, the National Hospital Workers Union. My parents could not afford to send my sister and me to camp until they found a camp in New Hampshire. The camp was run by the Church Master of an African Methodist Episcopal Church in Harlem whose pastor was the Reverend James Robinson, founder of Operation Crossroads Africa. My sister and I were not only the only Jews in the camp, we were the only whites who stayed the entire eight weeks.

I told the Speaker, "I did not know that whites were the majority until I was thirteen." Brown was hysterical. He had this infectious laugh that was heard throughout the restaurant.

He told me he had supported Alan Cranston in 1984, not Jesse Jackson. Jackson had approached a number of African American politicians who did not support him in 1984. Among them were Congressmen Mickey Leland of Texas, Bill Grey of Pennsylvania, Charlie Rangel of New York, and Mayor Harold Washington of Chicago.

Jackson had asked Willie Brown to be his National Campaign Chairman. Brown said he would only agree to the appointment if this campaign was serious and had a well-qualified campaign manager to whom Jackson would listen. Jackson agreed to the stipulation and asked Brown to find and hire that person. I told Brown, "A number of consultants must have said no." He answered that I was correct. He asked what it would take for me to accept the position. I responded that I must meet with Jackson. I could not accept the position without having a meeting with the candidate. He agreed. He told me to make sure I asked Maxine to arrange the meeting.

I met with Maxine and Danny Blakemore at a restaurant near LAX. Maxine was a legend. She was tough, she was smart, and she blew smoke right in your face. She agreed to set up the meeting for later in the week in New York. I returned to Columbus waiting to be summoned to New York to meet with Jackson. I was still undecided.

When I arrived at the hotel to meet Jackson, an aide escorted me to a waiting car and told me we were on our way to Wall Street to meet with managers of Merrill

Lynch. Jackson jumped in the back seat and proceeded to be briefed by two economists who would accompany him to his meeting.

Jackson wowed the Merrill Lynch folks and me. He was knowledgeable and confident in his presentation. We returned to the hotel and I was called to a private meeting with him.

He asked if we had ever met. I said yes, but doubted that he would remember. A year before, I was travelling west and changed planes in Chicago on my way to Los Angeles. The stewardess asked if I would move my seat.

I asked why and she said to accommodate two gentlemen who needed to sit next to each other. Jesse Jackson was one of those gentlemen. He did not remember but asked if he had thanked me. I said yes.

He told me that I had impressed Willie and Maxine and that the job was mine. I needed to work out the financial details with Willie. I told him I had not decided to take the job. I had a few questions which I needed answered. He said, "Fire away."

I told him I was Jewish. I wanted to know the derivation of "Hymie" and "Hymietown," his unfortunate statements from the 1984 campaign. I asked where it came from. He responded that when he was in the seminary in Chicago he and his friends would visit a restaurant called Hymie's. Because it was in the Jewish section of town, they referred to the area as "Hymietown." When he made the remark in 1984, he was accused of being anti-Semitic. The Jewish community in New York and nationally asked for an apology. Jackson said he'd been apologizing ever since.

I told him that whenever anyone uses a racial epithet, even if they do apologize, it says something about them. When someone uses the word "nigger," it says something about their upbringing and their values.

I asked him about his association with Louis Farrakhan. He said that Farrakhan had supported him in 1984. He does not subscribe to Farrakhan's philosophy but he also does not repudiate people.

I asked where he stood on a Palestinian homeland. He said he believed a Palestinian homeland was inevitable. I agreed, but added, "As long as it's not Israel."

After this conversation, I was still not persuaded to take the job. Jackson suggested that I travel with him for the next few days.

We traveled to Tulsa, Oklahoma, where Jesse was the main speaker at the Oklahoma AFL-CIO convention. Also on the schedule was a visit to an inner city high school.

The students were gathered in the gymnasium. As Jesse entered, a chant began softly and built into a crescendo. "Jes-ee, Jes-ee, Jes-ee." Jesse Jackson was more like a rock star than a politician. He was easily recognizable. He was known by one name, "Jesse," and he took over a room as soon as he entered.

After Jackson was introduced, he asked for the members of the boy's basketball team to come forward. After they joined him at the rostrum, he asked one of the players how much time each day he spent practicing basketball. The young man said, "Two hours with the team and another hour working on my own skills." Then Jackson asked, "And how much time each day do you spend studying?" The player hesitated and Jackson asked, "Four hours a day?" The athlete shook his head no. Jackson pushed on, "Three hours a day?" Again a shake of the head that said no. "Well," Jackson asked, "how much time do you spend each day studying?" The young man responded, "One hour." Jackson responded, "And during that one hour, are you talking to your girlfriend on the phone? Are you listening to the radio?" The young man nodded his head yes. Jackson asked the team to return to their seats.

Next he asked if there was a French teacher in the audience. A woman raised her hand and Jackson asked her to come down front. He hugged her and began to tell a story.

When he was in high school in Greenville, South Carolina, his mother insisted that he pursue an academic course of study which included a foreign language. He told his mother he didn't want to learn a foreign language. He'd never use it in Greenville. His protest fell on deaf ears. His mother signed him up for French. During his high school years he did the minimum to pass French, and when he graduated, he told the French teacher he would never, ever use French. When he enrolled in college, first at the University of Illinois and then at North Carolina A&T, he was required to take a foreign language. Again he chose French, and he did just enough to pass.

Years later, after he became famous, he was called by the Secretary General of the United Nations and asked to meet with a delegation of African ministers who were visiting Chicago. He agreed and the next day went to their hotel. To his surprise, all of these African leaders spoke as their native language, French.

Jackson ended his talk by leading those assembled in a recitation of "I am somebody."

I decided to accept the job. Not because I thought Jackson would win the nomination nor did I think Jackson would be President. I accepted the job because I believed that Jesse Jackson's calling was giving people hope. He encouraged, he cajoled, he influenced, he browbeat, and he led people to accomplishments they never thought they would experience.

I traveled to Tampa to meet Willie Brown at the airport to finalize the deal. Brown was in Tampa to speak to some association having their conference in the area. Willie's routine was to take the night flight from San Francisco east, catch a few hours' sleep, give his speech and return to California on the late afternoon plane.

Brown asked me how much I wanted to run the campaign.

I said, "$4,000 per month."

He said, "Dukakis' campaign manager gets paid $10,000 per month."

I responded, "Rich campaign, no message. We're a poor campaign, rich message."

"OK," he said, "What else?"

I responded, "I do all of the media."

He laughed and said, "Fine, but you won't have any money."

"Finally," I said, "I want the check book."

He laughed and said, "Here, it's all yours. I've been trying to get rid of this for months. Congratulations, you're $600,000 in debt."

"And one more thing," Brown cautioned, "only call me when you really need me. I have an assembly to run in California. I can't be bothered with day-to-day campaign decisions."

I laughed and told him, "Don't worry, you'll be calling me before I'll be calling you."

We wrote our agreement on a torn-off sheet of yellow lined paper and both signed it. When I last saw Willie Brown in 1995, when he was running for Mayor of San Francisco, he told me he still had that yellow piece of paper.

Branch Water and Bourbon

Tom Ingram

Senator Lamar Alexander tells this great story about Everett Dirksen, Republican Senator from Illinois and Lyndon Johnson. Dirksen had a great relationship with Lyndon Johnson from when he was Senate Minority Leader and Johnson was Senate Majority Leader in the 1950s.

Dirksen played a key role in helping President Johnson pass the Civil Rights Act of 1964 and 1968, and he was instrumental in rounding up support for Johnson's position on the Vietnam War.

Late one afternoon President Johnson calls Dirksen and says, "come on over and have a drink with me at the White House."

Dirksen, who was meeting with Lamar at the time, says, "I can't come over right now. I don't remember the last two nights in a row that I was at home. I've *got* to go home tonight." Lamar couldn't help but overhear the conversation.

Dirksen hangs up the phone and a few minutes later there was all this commotion in the hallway. It was the Secret Service clearing the hall for President Johnson.

If Dirksen couldn't go to Johnson, the president would come to him.

Back then it was not uncommon for senators to have a bar in their office and Dirksen was no exception.

Lamar left as Johnson and Dirksen retired to his private office for drinks—feeling certain that any legislative problems were about to be resolved over branch water and bourbon.

From Now On, He's With Me

Howie Carroll

I've really been around politics my entire life. My dad was a business agent for the window washers union and although he wasn't directly involved in politics, he was friendly with all the guys who were.

Over the years Dad became good friends with Richard J. Daley, the mayor of Chicago. As a business agent my dad had to negotiate contracts. In those days they weren't written contracts because everything was done through friendship and handshakes. That's how he became so friendly with Daley.

I still remember the first time I met Mayor Daley. It was 1954, when I was about twelve years old, and Daley was the Cook County Party Chairman. My dad asked me if I wanted to go to a political dinner with him and my mom. I said, "Sure, why not."

This was a huge Democratic fundraising dinner downtown at what was then the Sherman House. There were probably 1,500 or 2,000 people at the event. Technically you weren't supposed to hold the position of party chair and mayor at the same time, so Daley didn't announce for mayor until the end of 1954 *after* he was sworn in as party chair. He held both positions until the day he died.

Dad leaves our table and disappears for awhile, and when he comes back, he says, "How would you like to meet the next mayor of Chicago?"

In typical punk kid fashion, I say, "Why would *you* know the next mayor?"

He just says, "Come on Howie, he wants to meet you."

I walk with him out into the foyer, and there was a huge circle of people, and this little head pops up and Daley says, "Barney, is that Howie? I want to meet him."

The sea of people parts, and we walk in. Daley starts talking, telling me, "You know you're the same age as my Richie—you know we've got to get the two of you together—" And we're talking and talking, and then the bagpipes start.

He grabs me by the arm, and he says, come on, walk in with me. So I march into the room with him, *right down the center aisle*, and everybody's standing up cheering and screaming—this is not only the party chairman but the candidate for mayor.

Finally I tell him, "I better go sit down," and I returned to our table.

So Daley gets elected Mayor. One day my eighth grade teacher comes in and he says, "All right kids, Mayor Daley is coming out with a five-year plan, probably on Friday. When it comes out in the paper, I want you to have your parents cut it out, and bring it in to school so we can discuss it."

I go home and tell my dad what the teacher has asked us to do. The next day when he comes home Dad says, "You know him, why don't you just call his office and ask to see him to ask about it?" Dad gives me his phone number.

I figure, "Why not?" So I call and leave a message at the mayor's office. I go to school and later that day I get called down to the principal's office. I'm trying to figure out what I did to get in trouble. Instead the principal says, "The mayor's office is on the phone. He wants to talk to you."

All I can say is, "Oh, uh, ok, you know I met him at an event," like its nothing.

I take the phone and the mayor's office says he's making the announcement on Friday, and "could you be here at a quarter to twelve noon because he wants to see you before he makes the announcement."

So I turn to the principal, and ask her if it's ok if I go downtown to see the mayor at eleven forty-five on Friday because he wants to talk to me about the new plan he's coming out with.

The principal offers to drive me there but I tell her my dad can do that. So my dad and I go down to the mayor's office and all the press is waiting in the press area with those big old cameras.

We go in and sit down with Daley in his private office. He has two copies of his plan and signs both of them, one for me and one for my school. My dad and the mayor are kidding around, talking and telling jokes, while I'm thumbing through the plan which consisted of two books. The first was the text and the second listed the actual programs.

The mayor's watching me and he says, "Howie, what are you doing?" I keep thumbing through the plan, so he asks again, "Howie, what *are* you *doing*?"

I say, "I'm looking for the streets that I know to see what you're going to do in *my* neighborhood."

Then the mayor said, "Barney, you're right, this is a little politician. No one else would have done that. No one would have bothered to look."

And I say, "Well, I want to know what you're going to do." I must have had a quizzical look on my face because he then says, "What's the problem?"

"Well, Mr. Mayor, you know we're studying city government in school, and you were just elected to a four-year term *and this here is a five-year plan.*"

He starts laughing, and, you know, he had a great chuckle, and he says, "Well, what does that mean to you?"

I said, "Well, I see all these great programs, but I don't see when you're going to do them." And he says, "so . . ." and I say "you got elected for a four-year term, and this is a five-year plan, and if you don't do the streets in my neighborhood before the end of the first term, then you've got to be reelected so you can do them."

At this point, he's laughing so hard tears are coming to his eyes.

Finally he says, "Barney, this kid's a natural."

"It's like you said Howie, but nobody has caught on. It's the whole reason for the five-year plan—I didn't say I was gonna get to everything in the first four years. It may be in the plan for the fifth year. No one else has caught on yet."

He turned to my dad again, "Barney, you've got a smart little kid here. From now on he's with me!"

I saw a lot more of Daley after that as my dad took me to more political events and I became close to his son Richie, who eventually became mayor of Chicago as well.

Miss Anna Belle

Tom Ingram

Frank Clement, Democratic governor of Tennessee in the 1950s and 1960s, was a governor of some notoriety. He was known for his rousing sermon-like speeches and his support of integration. He was the first southern governor to veto a segregation bill.

His mission was mental health reform because he had mental health problems in his own family and he was going to make sure the mentally impaired of Tennessee were taken care of. Clement established the first mental health department in the state.

The governor's sister, Anna Belle Clement O'Brien, who passed away in 2009, was a character and politician in her own right.

She served as his chief of staff in the 1960s and went on to serve in the legislature for six years from 1975 to 1981.

Anna Belle was the governor's number one operative. If you wanted anything from Frank you had to go talk to Miss Anna Belle. She kept a file on every legislator. If a member of the legislature came to see her about a pet project, she would reach into her file drawer and retrieve their file.

She would then review the legislator's previous requests, saying, "Well let me see here," and she would list out every request they had made of the governor. "Now you have already asked us for this and this and this and you're asking me now for what?" She knew how every legislator had voted and what they had received from the administration.

There would be a little dialogue and then she'd say, "Now, we got this legislation coming up. Do you think you can help us out on that?" They would normally say "yes" and she would respond, "Well come back and see me about your request after you do." That was ultimate politics.

Miss Anna Belle was a political legend. I loved her. When she died a few years ago, I went to the visitation at her church in Crossville. I went up to the casket to pay my respects, and she's looking great, but there's a piece of corn bread in the casket.

So I go over to her niece and I ask her about the corn bread. She said, "Miss Anna Belle always said that if we thought she was dead to put a piece of corn bread in the casket, and if she didn't eat it, then she really *was* dead."

Great Storyteller

Nancy Korman

I met Speaker of the House of Representatives Tip O'Neill many, many times. As a matter of fact I have a picture of him in my living room with my son at a very young age, wearing a sweatshirt that says, "O'Neill Speakers," because that was the name of his softball team in Washington.

One evening Tip was doing an event for Paul Guzzi, who was running for secretary of state in Massachusetts, and my job was to take him around the Newton Armory and introduce him to people.

It was one of the most astounding experiences I have ever had, because I was about as necessary as a third wheel.

Tip knew absolutely everybody, everywhere. And he greeted them with incredible warmth.

He would walk up to people with a "Hello Joe, how's your mother doing, how's business," or a "Hello Sam, I heard your sister's sick." He just knew *everybody* and cared about what was going on in their lives.

Tip was totally down-to-earth and kind to everyone. He never made people feel uncomfortable. I think that's why he could reach across the aisle and do deals with Republicans.

Tip O'Neill was quintessentially Irish so he loved to tell stories. One of the stories that he told was about leaving Congress. When he left Congress, he had no money, absolutely no money because he had never hustled at all.

But Tip was an icon and very recognizable so he was offered all of these product endorsement opportunities. He liked to tell the story of how he was asked by Stove Top Stuffing to make an endorsement of their product. And his wife Millie said, "Tip, I really don't care who you speak on behalf of, but you've never eaten any stuffing except my homemade stuffing, so you can't do that."

He agreed to do American Express and he did a lot of others, but he never did Stove Top Stuffing and he never did a hair product because Millie said, "Who would ever believe you used one?"

A Story Left Untold

Jerry Austin

In 1988, I was retained by former Democratic Congressman James V. Stanton of Ohio to produce a video for his campaign for chairman of the Democratic National Committee.

The video eventually became a series of endorsements which included Congressman Dan Rostenkowski (D-Ill), Senator John Glenn, and Speaker of the House Tip O'Neill.

I would film interviews with each of the endorsers. I traveled to Boston to interview the Speaker. I brought along my copy of his book for the autograph.

After finishing the interview while the crew was breaking down the set, I asked the Speaker to autograph the book. As he was signing, I asked if there were any stories that were not in the book that he wished he had included. This is the story he told me.

In the 1970s when he was not yet Speaker but the Congressman from Cambridge, he hosted a book signing party for former Massachusetts Senator Leverett Saltonstall. Saltonstall, although a Republican, was an old friend of Tip's. The party was at Tip's law office and was well attended.

The Senator lived in Waltham and after the party, Tip asked if Saltonstall had a ride home. He said he'd take a cab. Tip suggested he have one of the summer law clerks drive him home, but Saltonstall said it was not necessary.

Tip insisted, telling the Senator that the young man would love to have the experience of spending forty-five minutes with such a famous Massachusetts politician. Saltonstall finally agreed. As they drove to Waltham, the young clerk asked many questions about famous politicians, such as John F. Kennedy and Henry Cabot Lodge. The Senator seemed to enjoy reminiscing.

As the call pulled into the Senator's driveway and pulled to a stop at the front door, the senator asked the clerk to wait until he returned. He wished to give him something to thank him for his kindness. The young man said that was not necessary. It was his honor to have spent this brief amount of time with the Senator.

Saltonstall responded, "Wait here, I'll be right back."

Five, ten, almost fifteen minutes passed and the clerk decided the Senator must have forgotten he was outside. As he started the car, the front door of the house opened and the senator walked out carrying a brown paper bag.

He opened the car door and handed the bag to the clerk and said, "Thank you very much. This is for you." The clerk said, "Thank you," and put the car in park as the Senator said, "Look at what's inside the bag." The clerk had expected an autographed copy of the Senator's book. What he found was a pound of frozen chop meat.

The clerk was speechless. The Senator said, "I know law school students do not have a lot of money. I thought you could use some good meat." He closed the car door and said, "Good night, young man."

I can still remember Tip laughing as he finished telling me the story. He said, "Can you believe it? A brown paper bag with a pound of frozen chop meat."

Justice and Power Politics

Steve Cobble

A few years ago, I had the privilege of accompanying Reverend Jesse Jackson on a trip to Europe. He was going to several cities and giving human rights lectures along the way. As I remember it, we stopped in Frankfurt, Germany, in Belgium, and in Amsterdam.

One of the highlights of the trip was a visit to the International Criminal Court (ICC) at The Hague, Netherlands. We were given a tour of their excellent facilities and treated very well that day. And Jesse was scheduled for a special meeting with a group of the judges at the end of the tour—a real honor.

Right before we went in, Jesse asked me what I thought he should bring up with the judges. I replied: "Well, the ICC does great work, but they don't have the political chops to take on the big countries when they violate human rights, so all their trials so far have been Balkan war criminals and African tyrants. They deserve it, but when are they going to bring Tony Blair before the court? When are they going to charge George W. Bush for war crimes?"

Jesse laughed, but sure enough, about an hour later, after four of the judges gave us a long and intelligent briefing on the ICC's history, principles, and current prosecutions, Jackson broke in: "But when are you going to charge Tony Blair for war crimes? You all know he's guilty."

There was a pause, a silence. Two of the judges were trying to stifle grins, while a third was having trouble not laughing out loud. The question had caught them all off guard, and everyone understood the obvious subtext—because of power politics, the ICC was only free to take on *some* war criminals, *not the strongest ones.*

The fourth judge bravely took on the delicate job of explaining that context to us, without saying it in a way that directly violated any institutional secrets.

Jackson sat there with a small smile on his face. The point had been made.

Coach Hayes and His Football Family

Jerry Austin

In 1981, I was retained by the Franklin County Democratic Party in Ohio to manage their council races. Three seats were up and the Democrats needed to retain all three seats to continue a majority on council.

Two of the candidates were incumbents. The third was Ben Espy, a first-time candidate and former football player at Ohio State University. Throughout the summer and fall, Ben was consistently running last in all polls, with three Democrats and three Republicans vying for three seats. The top three finishers would be declared the winners.

Ben was very smart and hardworking, but had very little name recognition. He was a former Ohio State football player that never became famous on the field.

As a senior in high school in Sandusky, Ohio, Ben was the number one running back in the state. He was heavily recruited by both Michigan and Ohio State universities. His hometown was equidistant between Columbus and Ann Arbor.

Ohio State Coach Woody Hayes sat in his living room and asked Ben where he had gone to elementary school. Ben wondered whether he meant the name of the school or the location. Woody asked again, "Which state did you live in while attending elementary school?" Ben sheepishly answered, "Ohio." And Hayes continued, "Where did you attend junior high and high school?" Again Ben responded, "Ohio."

Then Hayes asked Ben, "How can you be a traitor to your home state by attending that school up north?" Hayes referred to the University of Michigan as "that school up north." Ben decided to go to Ohio State. At age seventeen, he did not want to be known as a traitor.

I asked Ben if Coach Hayes would record a television commercial for him. He told me Hayes was a Nixon Republican and would never support a Democrat.

A week before the election Ben was involved in a minor traffic accident. While waiting for a tow truck, a former teammate stopped to see if he was OK. Ben said he was fine. Later that evening, the former teammate Greg Lashutka (presently the mayor of Columbus and a Republican) was talking to Coach Hayes on the phone. Greg told him Ben was in an auto accident but appeared to be fine.

The next day, Hayes called Ben at his office. I happened to be there at the time. Hayes asked Ben if there was anything he could do for him. Ben said no, he was fine. Ben hung up the phone and relayed the conversation to me.

I told him to call Hayes back and ask if he would cut a television ad for his campaign. Ben repeated that coach was a Nixon Republican and would never support a Democrat. I insisted he call. "Ben," I said, "You have nothing to lose." Reluctantly Ben called and to his surprise Coach Hayes responded he would be happy to do the ad.

That afternoon, I arrived with a crew at Hayes' office located in the ROTC building on the Ohio State University campus. Hayes had been fired as coach after striking a Clemson player during a bowl game of 1978. He had the title of Adjunct Professor of Military History.

As we waited for his arrival, I noticed a large stack of pink telephone messages. I nosily leafed through the messages and realized that almost every famous, and some not so famous, OSU football players had calls in to the old coach.

On the blackboard were titles of lectures. They included almost every battle of WWII.

Hayes arrived and I presented him with the script. He said, "Let's go—I'm ready." Then he mentioned for Ben to join him. He wanted Ben in the picture as he delivered his lines.

I said, "Coach—we only need you in this spot. If Ben is in the spot it takes away from your clout."

What I did not say was that I did not want Ben in the ad because Ben was black. His name was Ben Espy. I wanted the coach to talk about Ben and if people did not know who Ben was, they could think he was Italian. I did not want to give anyone any knowledge that they did not already have.

We completed the filming and before heading to the edit studio, I asked the coach if it was true that Hollywood was negotiating with him to film his life story. He said they had some preliminary talks. I asked who he would like to portray him in the film. He did not hesitate and answered, "Ed Asner."

I was dumbfounded and repeated, "Ed Asner, he's a very liberal Democrat." Hayes smiled and said, "He'd play me good."

As we were leaving I asked a final question of the coach. "Was this the first time you ever supported a Democrat for office?" I asked. He thought for a moment and responded, "I guess it is. But remember if you played for me, I don't care if you're a pro or a dishwasher, you will always be part of my family. And I'll do everything I can to help you."

The next Tuesday, Ben finished second in the election. On election day voters told reporters, "Woody told me to vote for Ben."

Campaigning for Lula

Steve Cobble

In the fall of 2002, Luiz Inácio "Lula" da Silva was on the verge of making history in Brazil. He was leading in the polls to become the first president of Brazil from the Workers Party, a political party he had helped start a generation before at direct risk to his life from the previous military dictatorship.

Through a former Jackson for President 1988 organizer, Carolyn Kazdin, who was now working with the Workers Party in Brazil, Jesse was invited to come down to meet Lula during the election. I was lucky enough to get to go with him.

It was a wonderful trip and one day in particular stands out as unbelievable. It was a Sunday, one week before the vote, and the last day for official campaigning under Brazilian election law.

We started the day with a friendly breakfast meeting with the mayor of São Paulo, Marta Suplicy, a very smart woman who had fought her way to the top of Brazilian politics. Halfway through the breakfast, a young man with needles through both cheeks came in with a similarly costumed female friend. It turned out that it was the mayor's son, Supla, a very popular punk rocker in Brazil.

After a couple of other good local events, we headed out to the soccer stadium for the final rally of the Workers Party. Brazilians are famous for knowing how to party, of course, but they are no slackers when it comes to stadium rallies either. It was an incredible event, with thousands and thousands of Workers Party supporters in the seats and on the field, waving huge flags, chanting, singing, clapping, and smiling.

I loved it and my friend James Gomez (Jackson's longtime foreign policy advisor) quickly decided to leave the stage area, and head down to the soccer field with the flags and bands and chanting. We wanted to be where the action was, and believe me, in more than forty years of campaigns, I've never seen anything like it.

A prominent state senator from the Workers Party came up to the microphone to thank Reverend Jackson for coming to visit. It turns out that he was Eduardo Suplicy, the ex-husband of the mayor of São Paulo we had met that morning, and the father of the punk rocker. He was so excited to have an actual figure from the American civil rights movement present at their last great pre-election rally that he decided to sing a song to honor the occasion: he burst out into a cappella version of "Blowing in the Wind" to the huge crowd in the stadium.

All at once it dawned on me. The crowd spoke Portuguese and he was singing the song in English. But it didn't seem to matter. He was no Peter, Paul, or Mary, and not even Bob Dylan for that matter, but the crowd was singing along, the flags were waving, and the crowd was happy, as I certainly was, to be along for the ride.

It was a great day for politics in Brazil. And the three members of that one family in São Paulo made it an unforgettable moment.

The Ballot Box Revolution

Jerry Austin

In 1986, I was a member of the international delegation that witnessed the Marcos/Aquino election in the Philippines.

After arriving in Manila and being briefed, I was assigned with my partner, the clerk of the legislature in Guinea, to the state of Illocos Norte. This was the Philippines' northernmost region and the home area of Ferdinand Marcos.

My partner and I arrived at the domestic air terminal at Manila International Airport two hours before flight time. We were told the flight was delayed. After two hours of waiting the airlines gave us vouchers for lunch and told us it would be an additional two hours until we boarded.

After six hours of waiting we boarded the plane, a twin prop with the pilot leaning his elbow out the window and wearing a "Terry and the Pirates" (an old comic strip character) hat, shades and a scarf.

The flight was very crowded and very bumpy. We were never more than ten thousand feet off the ground. When we finally arrived, we were met by a hired driver and driven into town to our hotel.

The one hotel in town was dingy, damp, and dirty. The communal bathroom had six inches of water covering the floor. A net hung around the bed to protect the guest from mosquitoes. The net had more holes than a piece of Swiss cheese.

After registering, we travelled a short distance to meet representatives of the two candidates and the election commission. They were intrigued by my New York accent and disturbed by my detailed questions about election day procedures.

I was thirsty and asked where I could get a cold beer. I was directed to an address which turned out to be the home of the Catholic Monsignor. I told him this was probably someone trying to play a joke on me. He said it was no joke. He had one of the few refrigerators in town and, yes, he had beer. He offered me a cold San Miguel which I accepted. While consuming the brew, the Monsignor asked if I would accompany him and his associates the next day and witness their vote. I agreed.

I asked if he was afraid of fraud. He said that in the last election, five years ago, Marcos received 100 percent of the vote. I was shocked. I never heard of a candidate receiving 100 percent of the vote even if this was his home area.

That evening we went to eat dinner at the only restaurant in town. The pièce de résistance was you picked out the chicken you wanted and, if interested, could watch it have its head chopped off and feathers plucked. We declined the invitation, but ate the chicken after it was cooked.

After dinner, we returned to the hotel and found the electricity off. We managed to climb in to our beds, but a very sleepless night followed. We had left instructions at the desk to wake us at five thirty a.m. so that we could be at the first polling we were to visit when it opened. We were awakened on time and sloshed our way in and out of the bathroom to take very quick, cold showers.

We drove to the first polling place and I reminded my partner that our instructions were to witness, not interfere. If we saw anything unusual, we were to write it down, period.

We arrived at the first polling place and I quickly noticed a tank at the side of the front door with a soldier in the cockpit.

We entered the polling place and introduced ourselves to the presiding judge. He welcomed us and told us what a great honor it was for him to meet us. Within minutes after our arrival, the Monsignor arrived with four other priests all dressed in their full battlefield regalia.

I greeted the Monsignor and his colleagues and was asked to witness each of their votes. A ballot was issued to each and they had to write the name of the candidate of their choice. I watched and witnessed each priest's vote for Aquino and their placing their individual ballot in to the assigned box. They thanked everyone and said they would return later for the official count.

We spent the remainder of the day travelling to polling places throughout the region. Every polling place had a military presence. At some a few soldiers stood guard, and at others they were accompanied by a tank. The crowds were large and orderly and we did not see any unusual occurrences.

We returned to the initial polling place with about ten minutes left before the polls were to be closed. I greeted the judge, who thanked me for returning. When the time came for the polls to close, the judge asked everyone to leave. He announced then he would have everyone reenter in about ten minutes and the count would commence. After waiting ten minutes, the judge opened the door and invited everyone back in to the polling place.

As I entered, he mentioned to me to come forward. I walked to where he was standing and he asked if I would open the ballot box. I agreed. He handed me a key and I placed it in the lock and opened the box. I started to walk away as the key was pulled from the box and the ballots read aloud.

Over the next half hour, he announced 179 votes for Marcos. I asked, violating my instructions, why each ballot for Marcos was in the same handwriting? He answered, "All of these voters are illiterate. We provide assistance for them. They tell my assistant for whom they want to vote and their vote is registered accordingly."

I pointed to the five Catholic priests and said, "I witnessed their vote. Every ballot they submitted was for Mrs. Aquino." He quickly responded, "Did you open the ballot box?" I answered, "Yes." "Did you witness each ballot was for Mr. Marcos?"

I said, "Yes." "And there were no more votes cast for Mrs. Aquino?" he asked. I said, "No." "Then," he said, "there were no votes cast for Mrs. Aquino." Instead of arguing further, I left the polling place and went outside to record what I had just heard and seen.

By the time we arrived back in Manila, a two-day trip because we had missed our once-a-day flight, the revolution had begun. Members of the delegation had reported similar incidences. A formal news conference was called and our delegation leaders presented our collective report to one of the largest assemblages of reporters I had ever seen.

By the time I arrived back in Columbus, the Aquino forces had seized the state-owned television station and the Marcoses were on their way to Hawaii.

Comrade Steve

Steve Cobble

Because of my work for the Jesse Jackson for President 1988 campaign, I had the incredible honor of being chosen to travel to South Africa in 1991. I had been asked to help conduct get-out-the-vote training for the African National Congress as they prepared for the first democratic elections in the nation's history. Nelson Mandela had been freed from prison the year before. Political, cultural, and racial changes were on the march, and now the activists and protestors needed to get ready for campaign politics.

In a large hotel room in Bloemfontein, South Africa, the city where the organization that eventually became the ANC was founded just over a century ago, several of us made presentations to the several hundred young organizers who made up the crowd. (I was only about forty years old then, but I was twice as old as most of the audience.)

After the presentations we broke down into workshops, and I led one on GOTV, which seemed to go well. When we reconvened in the big hall, each group reported back to the main body.

The "reporter" for my workshop gave a good recap and had the generosity to keep referring to me as "Comrade Steve" whenever he mentioned some pearl of wisdom I had said. For a middle-class white boy, at the time living in Grinnell, Iowa, getting called "Comrade Steve" repeatedly by ANC organizers felt pretty damn good.

While I was basking in my revolutionary solidarity, the reports ended, and one young teenager asked if he could read a poem he had just written in honor of this great day of training. He came up to the front, and started delivering the poem, mostly in Afrikaans, which I, of course, do not speak, but with some English sprinkled in.

After the second or third chorus, I noticed a couple of the other trainers looking over at me and grinning. All at once it dawned on me—the chorus of this poem was essentially, "Kill all the white farmers!"

Since I was listed on the program as living in Iowa—a famous farm state—and since the only other white in the whole hall was a Bulgarian, it began to dawn on me that I was the closest thing to a "white farmer" in the room, even though I was more or less completely ignorant of farm life.

The poem soon ended, and I went back to being "Comrade Steve," but the symbolism of my skin remained, and my training partners had a good time teasing me the rest of the week.

On the Road to Belfast

Jerry Austin

After spending a day in New York on business, I headed to Kennedy Airport for my nine p.m. British Airways flight to London. There, after a seven-hour flight and going through customs and a short layover, I would board a British Airways flight to Belfast.

First decision: how to get to Kennedy? As a native New Yorker, I know all the choices: (1) bus, (2) cab, (3) subway to bus, or (4) relative or friend. I eliminated choices (3) and (4) quickly, and finally settled on number 1. I would be leaving near the end of rush hour, but the $8 bus ride was a bargain.

I boarded the bus in front of the City Squire Hotel on 7th Avenue and 51st Street. After a twenty-minute ride, I arrived at Grand Central Station where I transferred to another bus for the ride to Kennedy. Coincidently, all of the passengers of the bus were headed for international flights. As luck would have it, the British Airways terminal was the last stop. I exited from the bus one hour and five minutes after boarding.

At the British Airways first-class check-in counter (I always travel first class when consulting overseas), I was informed that all non-smoking seats were taken. I was told that my travel agent had not reserved a non-smoking seat. I protested that I could not and would not sit in the smoking section for the seven-hour trip to London. The gate agent asked if I would consider taking the delayed Concorde flight also leaving at nine p.m.—non-smoking seats were available.

I have travelled on the Concorde on two other occasions, both times from London to JFK. The thought of a three-hour flight instead of a seven-hour flight was very appealing and I accepted her offer.

I waited in the first class lounge, where I was more interested in watching the first half hour of the Cards-Giant playoff game than eating and drinking all the free grub. But as luck would have it, only one TV set was available and a British couple was into some Tuesday night sitcoms. I went downstairs to the hoi polloi bar and watched the top of the first inning before my Concorde flight was called to board.

The Giants scored a run in the top of the first and I was off to London and Belfast hoping when I returned the Giants would be in the World Series. You may ask, why a Giants fan? I grew up in the South Bronx in the mid-forties to the mid-sixties. I was the only kid in my neighborhood that was not a Yankee fan. My first sports memory was in 1951. I ran from school at PS 75 to Kreage's on Westchester Avenue and pushed my way to the front of the crowd watching the Giants-Dodgers playoff game. As I arrived in front of the TV, Bobby Thompson stepped to the plate. My first sports memory was "the shot heard round the world." From that day, I became and remained a Giants fan (when I'm not also rooting for the Mets).

I landed at London Heathrow at 5:10 in the morning, three hours and nine minutes after leaving JFK at an average speed of over 1100 miles per hour. At 5:18 in the morning, there are no lines through customs. My one bag arrived quickly and I headed for the transfer desk to check my bag at Belfast. Nice try! You have to check Belfast bags at the domestic terminal because all Northern Ireland bags go through a special security check. I was told to board a shuttle bus and head to Terminal 1.

I boarded the shuttle bus and journeyed through a labyrinth of roads and gates, finally arriving at Terminal 1. At six a.m., security was closed until seven. Not to worry, I'd change some money while I was waiting—of course, the money exchange was not open until seven a.m.

So I sat in the terminal and watched Londoners board shuttle flights to Glasgow, Edinburgh, and Dublin like Comair commuters going to Cleveland, Cincinnati, and

Indianapolis. At seven thirty a.m., I decided to call my Belfast contact Alex Attwood, Belfast City councilor and campaign manager for the council elections to be held October 22nd.

I entered the telephone booth and was baffled by the instructions. I wanted to use my AT&T credit card but I couldn't find any instructions. I called the operator and was told I could not use my international credit card to call Belfast because Belfast was part of the United Kingdom. However, I could use my Visa or Master-Card at the appropriate machine. I finally found a credit card telephone and informed Alex of my early arrival.

I was met at Belfast International Airport and was driven to the Europa Hotel. Before entering the hotel, I had to go through security. The Europa Hotel is the most bombed hotel in Europe. Luckily, it hasn't been bombed for six years.

My first appointment was with Dr. Joe Hendron, the Socialist Democratic Labor Party's candidate for Parliament against Gerry Adams of Sinn Fein (IRA). Hendron had lost to Adams in 1983 by 5,000 votes and in June by 2,200. Dr. Joe, as he's called, first wanted to talk about the recent European victory over the United States in the Ryder Cup. I told him I had attended a round and he was eager to hear my eyewitness account. On to more serious business—Hendron thought one of the reasons he lost was fear. Many SDLP voters stayed home. They stayed away not for lack of interest, but because they believed if Sinn Fein lost, West Belfast would be terrorized by the IRA.

This belief startled me. I had remembered being horrified when I saw soldiers with M-16 rifles standing in front of the polling places in the Philippines. Hendron and Attwood told me of their cars being stolen and set on fire. On more than one occasion, he had his office windows broken by bricks. I was impressed by the passion and dedication of the SDLP members I met at their annual conference in New Castle. I didn't realize how brave they were too.

Alex next took me on a tour of West Belfast—a neighborhood that reminded me of my native South Bronx. West Belfast is a lower- and middle-class area divided into Lower Falls and Upper Falls. The Lower Falls consisted of public housing complexes; Upper Falls was middle class with private homes in the $35,000-$50,000 range.

The election on October 22 was to fill two seats vacated by incumbent councilors. The incumbents were members of the Unionist Party. The Unionists were loyal to England. The SDLP were the moderates seeking the middle ground between those loyal to England and the IRA, which advocated a removal of British troops from Northern Ireland.

That evening, I joined Alex and a group of Queens University students canvassing Upper Falls. The residents were just getting over the parliamentary elections in June and were not aware there was a special election on October 22nd. Many of the residents whispered they were SDLP and quickly closed the door. One of the major issues in the area was the lack of a community center that catered to the needs of the neighborhood. Alex was heartened by the recognition given to the SDLP Advice Center which opened during April. The center was staffed six days a week by the three SDLP councilors and volunteers.

The next day, I met with the two SDLP candidates for the West Belfast council seats. Gerry Cosgrove, a thirty-five-year-old mother and longtime party worker, lived with her husband, Mervyn, in one of the unending Lower Falls row houses. Gerry was a first-time candidate who had been a secretary at SDLP headquarters for years. Her husband had been unemployed for eight years and took care of the house and children while Gerry worked. Gerry spoke of the widespread fraud that exists during elections. An ID card is necessary to prove who you are at the voting booth. However, a picture is not required. Gerry reported the IRA had been calling into West Belfast and asking residents if they had ID cards. It was assumed that whenever they were told no, a potential fraudulent vote was possible.

I asked why this practice was not stopped? Gerry stated she feared her children would be kidnapped or her husband beaten up if she spoke out. She was a nervous wreck for two weeks fearing repercussions. Although none took place, she did not want to go through the same experience.

Gerry Cosgrove was well liked in her community but given little chance of succeeding because of the IRA strength in Lower Falls. The Upper Falls candidate was Gerry Kelly, a father and teacher who lived in a decent middle-class home in Upper Falls. Gerry had been working hard and was cautiously optimistic. Kelly believed he'd taken a big chance running for office. Negative repercussions might be felt at the school level. It could mean the loss of promotion. Why was he taking this chance? He lost a friend recently—he believed—killed by IRA henchmen. He decided he had to do something. Over the objections of his wife, he entered the council race.

Kelly and Attwood believed if the SDLP can win one of the two West Belfast seats, and win another seat in the 1989 elections, they could defeat Adams and the IRA in 1991. The only IRA seat in Parliament is the West Belfast seat.

It's hard to believe—Adams and the IRA won the seat in 1983, but Adams has never been sworn in and has never attended a session in Parliament. Winning the seat and not being sworn in is the IRA's form of protest.

The SDLP held three parliamentary seats: John Hume from Derry elected in 1983 and reelected in 1987; Seamus Mailler elected in 1986 and reelected in 1987; and Eddie McCratty, who beat Enoch Powell in 1987.

The SDLP was a relatively young party—less than twenty years old. They formed as a compromise between the Protestant, pro-England Loyalists and the Catholic, terrorist IRA. The SDLP is overwhelmingly Catholic and believes the English will only leave the North when the people of the North unite.

On my last day in Belfast, I met with student leaders at Queens University, one of the four state colleges in the North. Students compete for entrance into Queens, and they are given stipends for tuition and room and board.

For the past eight years, most of the student union presidents were active SDLP members. The union president is elected by the eight thousand students to a one-year term. The president oversees the operation of the union, which consists of a bookstore, three cafeterias, a travel agency, and an insurance company. The budget is 1.4 million pounds per year. The students were very interested and knowledgeable about U.S. presidential politics. Many of them had attended a National Democratic Institute Seminar in DC in 1985 and were very impressed with Joe Biden and Al Gore. Their number one question was who would be the next president of the United States? The students at Queens were the main volunteers for the West Belfast campaign.

Before leaving Belfast, I visited DBA Associates, the media production firm responsible for all party media production in the 1985 parliamentary elections in Northern Ireland. The television networks BBC One and Two provided the same amount of air time for all political parties—a three-minute spot for the party and a two-minute spot for each candidate. The spots are aired only during the last two weeks of the campaign. The facilities were more modern than I envisioned. I viewed the videos of all the parties. They were simple and not very inspiring. Although the air time was free, the parties paid for production of their videos. During this special election, there will not be any television time provided by the networks. All advertising will be done in the newspaper, via quarter- and half-page ads.

As always, I had learned much more from my visit to Belfast than I taught. I worked on free media ideas, themes, and newspaper ads but my most rewarding experience came from the SDLP members I met. We in the United States take so much for granted. Our freedoms, although only two-hundred-plus years young, have not been realized by my friends in Northern Ireland. Personal danger was a way of life, British police patrols were the norm, and fraud-free elections were almost nonexistent.

Their one hope is the young people. They are committed to peaceful change reminiscent of the civil rights and anti-war movement in America. As one senior citizen told me, "I hope the young people can make the changes necessary and I hope I'll be alive to see it."

The Ostrich Has Landed

Wayne Johnson

One day I had a gentleman show up on my doorstep in California to ask for advice on dealing with the regime under which he lived in Africa. He got my name from a fellow in a neighboring country that had heard me speak at a conference in yet a third African nation.

That initial conversation eventually led to contact with the opposition leadership, who invited us in for a visit. I had worked with Felipe Noguera, the brilliant Argentine strategist on various projects and recruited him to help.

Felipe was no stranger to working in dangerous places and was currently involved in an election in a Latin American country noted for election violence. He would catch a flight from Central America and advise me when he made it to Miami.

Given the unstable political situation on the ground, we had decided to meet up in Miami where I would give Felipe his cover documents. We would be ostrich leather merchants.

I remember the typically droll email I received when Felipe arrived in Miami. It said simply, "The ostrich has landed." I always thought that would be a good title for a book about international political consulting, capturing the combination of the fascinating, surreal, and absurd.

As we entered the country's airspace on the last leg of the trip, we disposed of anything that could make us look the least bit political in the airplane lavatory. We tried to look appropriately dour as we suspected ostrich leather merchants would look.

Once in the country, we took another flight to a more remote area, arriving after dark. We were greeted outside the airport by a gentleman who would then drive us some distance to where we would meet with opposition leaders the following day.

Driving in many parts of Africa is not recommended after dark, simply because too many things can end up in the middle of the road, while other roads simply end without warning.

We noticed that we were tooling along, not only after dark, but without the benefit of headlights. For those who have visited Buenos Aires, they will be familiar with the common practice of taxis often driving downtown without headlights at night. They claim it's easier for them to see.

Felipe mentioned this to our driver and asked if that was the reason we were zooming along in the dark.

"Oh, no," he said cheerily. "I'm number three on the new death list they put out today, so trying not to make it easy for them."

The People Vote No

Jerry Austin

In 1988, I was a member of the international delegation witnessing the Pinochet plebiscite in Chile.

General Augusto Pinochet had led the overthrow of former President Salvator Allende and installed himself as President and Commander in Chief of the Armed Forces.

The reform movement had pushed for a referendum to decide whether the president and commander-in-chief could be the same person. The correct vote for the reformers was "NO."

In October 1987, the date for the votes was scheduled for the following October of 1988. In 1987, no one in the country was registered to vote. There had not been an election in the eighteen years Pinochet had been dictator. A serious registration campaign was designed and implemented. By the time election day approached, 94.7 percent of eligible voters registered.

I arrived in Santiago, one of the most beautiful and most European cities in South America, two days before the election. In Chile, as in the Philippines, all electioneering ends forty-eight hours before election day. And as in the Philippines, the last activity is a massive rally in the largest city in the country. We arrived at our hotel at the end of the final "NO" rally attended by a million people.

The next day, the day before the election, we were briefed and given our assignments. I was assigned to stay in Santiago.

At one of the briefings, we were informed that both sides of the issue were given one hour of television time to be used before the election. They could choose to use the entire hour at once or break it up into thirty-second spots or a combination.

We asked to see the spots of the "NO" campaign. First, we were shown a spot which was an attempt to re-educate the populace. The spot was a resumé of the atrocities of the Pinochet regime. We were told the spot was not very effective. Next we were shown the spot that changed the expected win for the "YES" side to an expected win for the "NO" side.

The spot opened with a distance view of a deserted street. As the camera moved in, you saw a car sitting under a lamp post. In the front seat, sat a young couple. The young man puts his arm around the young woman and begins to place his hand inside her blouse. She pushes his hand away and says "NO." That's it; that's the spot. Everyone remembered this spot and the exclamation "NO."

On election day we arrived at the first polling place, the soccer stadium where Allende was assassinated. Thirty-five thousand people were eligible to vote at this location. When we arrived, we observed Air Force personnel out in force. We were told they were there for crowd control. I thought back to the Philippines and was immediately leery of this explanation. It proved to be true.

Chileans had not voted in eighteen years and many of those voting that day had never voted in their life. We witnessed long lines at the soccer stadium as well as every polling place we visited. By noon, half the polling places in the country had a 100 percent turnout of registered voters.

The final result had the "NO" side winning. Ninety-seven percent of eligible voters participated. But my most lasting memory was the huge throngs of people who after voting lined up across the street from the polling place. They were dressed in their Sunday best. They watched silently as their countrymen voted, as if they were at a religious event. Most of them had never voted and they wanted the moment to last.

It seems to me that what the United States requires to increase turnout is ten to twenty years of a dictatorship. If we lost what we take for granted, we might appreciate what we have.

About the Contributors

Jerry Austin has been one of the nation's most experienced and successful political strategists. Austin has consulted on races throughout the United States at every level from precinct committee person to President of the United States. Raised in the Bronx, Austin learned his politics in Cleveland in the late 1960s. After helping elect Richard Celeste Governor of Ohio twice, he became the campaign manager for Reverend Jesse Jackson's 1988 presidential campaign. He was the senior political director for Paul Tsongas's 1992 campaign for president and helped elect Paul Wellstone to the United States Senate. In 1992, he was the consultant and media advisor for Carol Moseley Braun's historic campaign for the U.S. Senate. His work also includes witnessing the Marcos/Aquino election in the Philippines; the Pinochet plebiscite in Chile; and many trips to Northern Ireland to consult for the SDLP party. Mr. Austin earned a BA in American History from the City College of New York; a Masters in Public Administration from New York University; and a Masters in Education from the University of Akron. He is currently an Adjunct Professor and Director of the International Campaign Fellows program at The Bliss Institute of Applied Politics at The University of Akron.

Howie Carroll grew up in West Rogers Park, the son of Barney Carroll, a business agent for the window washer's union and a Democratic Party operative. Howie was twenty-seven and a lawyer when he was tapped by local committeemen to run for the Statehouse. Two years later he was elevated to the Senate, where he's been ever since, making him Illinois' longest-serving senator.

Steve Cobble was the national delegate coordinator for Jesse Jackson for President 1988 and later served as political director for the National Rainbow/PUSH Coalition. He also cofounded Progressive Democrats of America, the organization that started the "draft Bernie" effort more than two years ago and the first national organization to endorse Sanders for President.

Stephen Ira "Steve" Cohen is the U.S. Representative for Tennessee's 9th congressional district which includes almost three-fourths of Memphis. Steve is a member of the Democratic Party and is Tennessee's first Jewish congressman.

Paul Curcio has written and produced advertising for candidates in every region of the country at every level from president to mayor. Paul began his political career at the National Republican Senatorial Committee in 1984. Paul was an adjunct instructor at the George Washington University and was a visiting fellow at the Bob Dole Institute of Politics at the University of Kansas.

Dale Emmons is a Kentucky-based Democratic political professional who founded the firm Emmons & Company, Inc. in 1990. Dale has a remarkable record of business success and of winning and has been part of more than 650 winning political campaigns. Dale has served on the Democratic National Committee and the DNC Executive Committee.

Peter Fenn is president of Fenn Communications Group, one of the nation's premier political and public affairs media firms. Prior to forming the firm, Peter was the first Executive Director of Democrats for the 80s, which was a political action committee. Peter also served on the staff of the Senate Intelligence Committee and as Washington Chief of Staff for Senator Frank Church.

Jim Friedman has provided legal counsel to clients in challenging legal, financial, and business matters for more than forty years. His in-depth knowledge of the banking industry and his creative approach to navigating legal issues have allowed him to assemble teams of lawyers to handle countless legal matters including business litigation, securities offerings, mergers and acquisitions, labor and employment, tax, employee benefits, and more.

Dave Heller is one of the top political media consultants and campaign strategists in the Democratic Party. As president of Main Street Communications, an award-winning political media firm, Dave has compiled the best won-loss record in the Democratic Party helping clients win elections to Congress.

Alice Huffman is President and CEO of her consulting firm A.C. Public Affairs, Inc. (ACPA) which specializes in initiative campaigns, strategic public policy issues, and grassroots organizing. ACPA, founded in 1988, has many distinguished national and state clients. Alice was also President of the California NAACP.

Tom Ingram founded the Ingram Group after leaving his post as Deputy to the Governor and Chief of Staff to then-Governor Lamar Alexander. Tom realized if he could do anything, he'd hang a shingle and put up a sign that said "Crisis manager, problem solver." He did just that in Nashville in 1983.

Wayne Johnson serves as the President of The Wayne Johnson Agency, a nationally recognized political and public affairs firm, and has served as a senior consultant on more than two hundred and fifty candidate campaigns. He is also the former president of the American Association of Political Consultants, an association which represents more than one thousand political and public affairs professionals. Wayne also served as an American representative on the Board of Directors of the International Association of Political Consultants.

Robert "Bob" Keefe serves as the President of TKC International, Inc., a Washington, DC-based government relations and public affairs firm founded in 1978. Bob is a longtime veteran of Democratic Party politics and has served as an advisor to presidential candidates, senators and congressmen, governors, and mayors. He writes regularly at www.bobkeefedc.com as well as lecturing on politics and trade policy and is a regular speaker at business forums and corporate meetings.

Tom King is a former DCCC political director who has been involved in over two hundred elections ranging from state representative and mayoral races all the way to the U.S. Senate. Tom started Tom King Communications to provide a personalized service to a small group of clients. Tom previously worked for Boston Mayor Kevin White.

Nancy Korman established a marketing communications and graphic design firm called 760 Associates in 1970. Nancy wrote a weekly column for the *Boston Herald* which focused on social issues and the role of women in contemporary society. She also served as the Chair of the Massachusetts Service Alliance for ten years.

Bill Lacy is a former political operative and business executive who is the current Director of the Bob J. Dole Institute of Politics and was the campaign manager for Fred Thompson's 2008 presidential campaign. Bill has served in various positions within the Republican National Committee and has worked on many presidential campaigns and administrations.

Bob Mulholland is a California-based political activist. He was a senior advisor to the California Democratic Party from 1991 to 2010. From 1992, he was a political consultant to Tony Blair and the Labour Party (UK).

Steve Murphy has worked to elect Democrats since 1976 when he started with the Jimmy Carter for President Campaign. Steve also served as Executive Director of the U.S. House Democratic Caucus. He has worked with many governors, senators, members of Congress, mayors, and constitutional officers.

Richard Norman has served as the President of The Richard Norman Company, a fundraising and communications agency for candidates, nonprofit organizations, and PACs to help Republicans across the United States, since 1987. Through his company, Richard has managed fundraising programs for well-known organizations and candidates for president, U.S. Senate, House of Representatives, and governor. He is also the founder of Patriot Data Services, a computer service agency, and ActiveEngagement, a digital communications and fundraising agency.

Jeff Plaut is a founding partner of the Global Strategy Group, a public affairs agency whose clients include Democratic Party candidates and office holders. His approach to helping clients win elections and major advocacy efforts led him to be known as one of the top Democratic pollsters in the country.

John Rendon, CEO and President of the Rendon Group, is recognized internationally as an experienced and innovative strategic communications planner and operator. John began his career as an election campaign consultant to Democratic Party politicians. Considered an authority on the real-time global information environment, John lectures on strategic communications, international campaign management, and crisis management at universities worldwide.

Rick Rendon is the cofounder and Senior Partner of The Rendon Group, Inc. He has served as event producer or manager for over 250 special events during his career. These events include: the Aruban Democratic Party "AVP" Convention and the Massachusetts Democratic State Convention. In addition to having more than twenty-five years of experience as a senior communications consultant, Mr. Rendon previously served as a Public Information Officer for the Secretary of the Commonwealth of Massachusetts, and as a member of United States President Jimmy Carter's national political staff.

Karen T. Scates has provided expertise in strategic marketing and communications and public relations. Karen has been counsel to a variety of organizations creating targeted, effective messages to meet business objectives. She has used digital marketing and social channels to create effective branding to meet growth objectives.

Rick Schlackman began his political career in California as a member of the field staff on statewide and local political races. Rich is the longest-serving Democratic board member on the American Association of Political Consultants and recently received their Lifetime Achievement Award. He is widely credited as a leader in working to professionalize the field of political consulting.

Ace Smith is a thirty-year veteran of state and national politics and has directed winning campaigns from district attorney to president. With deep experience on the West Coast, Ace specializes in high-stakes political, governmental and public affairs campaigns. He also has extensive experience advising corporate clients and winning complex initiative campaigns.

Garry South, principal of the Garry South Group, has nearly forty years of experience at high levels in government, politics and business consulting. Garry has worked for both the federal government and state governments in three different states and has managed or played leading roles in numerous campaigns. He served as Midwest Regional Finance Director of the Democratic National Committee and is a specialist in the political use of radio.

Doc Sweitzer is one of The Campaign Group's founders and is a veteran of two presidential campaigns. Doc has successfully elected more than thirty members of Congress and statewide elected officials. He brings a special expertise in media targeting and is a regular guest lecturer across the country on political strategy and media planning.

J. Warren Tompkins has had an enduring impact on South Carolina politics for nearly three decades. Highly regarded as a shrewd political strategist, his advice has been sought throughout the Southeast in local, state, and national races. At First Tuesday

Strategies, Warren has acted as a head consultant to various state and local level campaigns.

John Toohey serves as Director of Strategy for LG Electronics where he is responsible for strategic planning and corporate development. Prior to joining LG Electronics, John was a Director in the mergers and acquisitions department of UBS Investment Bank where he advised clients on over twenty-five announced transactions, representing approximately $21 billion across a wide range of healthcare sectors and other industries.

Frank Watkins is a democratic political operative who is best known for serving as a chief advisor to Reverend Jesse Jackson's campaign for President. He was hired as campaign manager for Reverend Sharpton, who adopted the "progressive partisan" political ideology of Representative Jesse Jackson Jr., which was penned by Mr. Watkins.